VOCABULARY WORKSHOP

LEVEL ORANGE

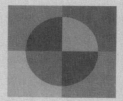

Teacher's Annotated Edition

With Answers to Tests (Cycles One and Two)

SADLIER-OXFORD

A Division of William H. Sadlier, Inc.

New York, NY 10005-1002

VOCABULARY WORKSHOP

THE CLASSIC PROGRAM FOR:

- developing and enriching vocabulary resources
- promoting more effective communication in today's world
- improving vocabulary skills assessed
  on standardized tests

S is a registered trademark of William H. Sadlier, Inc.

Printed in the United States of America
ISBN: 0-8215-0414-2
3456789/01 00 99

CONTENTS

Introduction iv
Overview of the Program v
Guide to the Student Text viii
Guide to the Supplementary Testing Program xiii
Implementing the Program xiv
Planning Chart xiv
Weekly Lesson Plans xvi
Alternate Approaches xix
Classroom Techniques xxi
Alternate Types of Assessment xxii
Teacher Resources xxiii
Answers to Analogies in Student Text Reviews xxiv
Answers to Testing Program Cycle One xxv
Answers to Testing Program Cycle Two xxix

ANNOTATED STUDENT TEXT

Foreword 4
The Vocabulary of Vocabulary 5
Pronunciation Key 9
Diagnostic Test 10
Unit One 12
Unit Two 18
Unit Three 24
Unit Four 30
Review (Units One–Four) 36
Unit Five 42
Unit Six 48
Unit Seven 54
Unit Eight 60
Review (Units Five–Eight) 66
Cumulative Review I (Units One–Eight) 72
Unit Nine 76
Unit Ten 82
Unit Eleven 88
Unit Twelve 94
Review (Units Nine–Twelve) 100
Unit Thirteen 106
Unit Fourteen 112
Unit Fifteen 118
Unit Sixteen 124
Review (Units Thirteen–Sixteen) 130
Cumulative Review II (Units Nine–Sixteen) 136
Final Mastery Test 140
Index 144

INTRODUCTION

Over the last five decades VOCABULARY WORKSHOP has become the "classic" program for

- guiding and stimulating vocabulary growth in Grades 6–12;
- preparing students in those grades for vocabulary-related exercises found in tests.

Level Orange, one of two new additions to the VOCABULARY WORKSHOP series

- extends the program to students in the upper elementary grades, and increases the range of levels suitable for use by middle school students;
- faithfully maintains the approach that has made VOCABULARY WORKSHOP so beneficial;
- introduces new features to keep abreast of changing times and changing testing procedures, particularly in regard to standardized tests.

This Teacher's Edition for Level Orange of VOCABULARY WORKSHOP is designed to help teachers make effective use of the program in the classroom.

- Part I furnishes teachers with an overview of the goals, grade placements, and pedagogical approach of the VOCABULARY WORKSHOP program.
- Part II familiarizes teachers with the Student Text and Supplementary Testing Program for this level and outlines a plan for the integrated use of these items during the school year.
- Part III provides practical suggestions for effectively implementing the program in the classroom.

OVERVIEW

Goals

The goals of the VOCABULARY WORKSHOP program are threefold:

- developing and enhancing student vocabulary resources;

- promoting more effective communication, both oral and written, in today's world;

- improving vocabulary-related skills assessed on standardized tests.

Grade-Level Placement

Level Orange has been conceived with the fourth grader in mind, Level Blue with the fifth grader.

In determining "proper" placement of either level in a given situation, however, the following considerations should be taken into account:

- Grade levels indicated should not be taken in too literal or rigorous a sense. A certain amount of experimentation, as well as the use of the Diagnostic Test, are needed to establish the "correct" placement of a particular level in a given situation.

- Both Levels Orange and Blue have been prepared in such a way as to offer *some* students in grades 6 and 7 with material as challenging, though different in format, as the first two levels of the VOCABULARY WORKSHOP Levels A–H.

- Differences in grade are reflected not only in the "difficulty" of the words presented but also in the "maturity" of the sentences and other contexts in which those words are used.

Pedagogical Approach

VOCABULARY WORKSHOP features a *balanced approach* to word acquisition.

- This approach focuses primarily on the words themselves, their meanings, their ranges of application (applicability), and their relationships to other words.

- At the same time, the approach recognizes the importance of textual *context* in the acquisition of vocabulary and in its proper usage.

One of the cornerstones of the pedagogical approach taken in VOCABULARY WORKSHOP is intensive reinforcement through varied and abundant "hands-on" exercises. This method of teaching vocabulary is emphasized to provide students with

- maximum exposure to different meanings of the key words studied;

- maximum coverage of the range of applicability of each key word through its application in the greatest possible number of different contexts;

- fullest understanding of a key word's relationships to other words.

Although it is customary to say that a student does or does not "know" a particular word, it should be recognized that there are actually many levels of word recognition and control.

These levels range from complete nonrecognition to partial or complete recognition *in context only* to the full incorporation of a word in a student's active vocabulary.

The aim of the instructional material and exercises presented in VOCABULARY WORKSHOP is to move the word into the students' active daily-use vocabulary.

A Consumable Program

A major feature of this program is that the students are directed to write answers directly in the book. This technique was designed to

- help students learn to spell the key words properly;
- ensure active student participation in the program;
- build a permanent record of student work.

Word Lists

The Student Texts for Levels Orange and Blue each contain 192 key words, divided over 16 Units.

Criteria for Selection

The selection of words was based on four major criteria:

- currency in and usefulness for present-day American oral and written communication;
- frequency on recognized vocabulary and spelling lists;
- applicability to standardized tests;
- current grade-placement research.

General Sources

The lists of key words were developed from many sources:

- traditional, classic, and contemporary fiction and nonfiction, including novels, short stories, biographies, essays, newspaper and magazine articles, plays, films, videos, TV programs;
- spelling and vocabulary lists recognized as valid bases for teaching language skills;
- current subject-area textbooks, glossaries, and ancillary materials (especially for general, nontechnical terms).

Dictionary and Reference Sources

The following were the primary dictionary resources used for word (and definition) selection:

- *Webster's Third International Dictionary of the English Language* (unabridged);
- *Merriam-Webster's Collegiate Dictionary* (tenth edition).

Other dictionary reference works consulted include:

- *The American Heritage Dictionary of the English Language* (all three editions);
- *The Random House Dictionary of the English Language* (unabridged; both editions);
- *The Compact Edition of the Oxford English Dictionary.*

In addition, a number of other word finders or reference works were utilized in preparing the drill, testing, reinforcement, or enhancement materials.

Standard Word-Frequency Sources

Standard word-frequency studies were employed to evaluate and revise the words on the tentative lists. These include:

Dale-O'Rourke: *The Living Word Vocabulary*

Carroll-Davies-Richman: *Word Frequency Book*

Zeno-Ivens-Millard-Duvvuri: *The Educator's Word Frequency Guide*

Harris-Jacobsen: *Basic Reading Vocabularies*

In compiling word lists, every effort has been made to include only such words as, according to authorities consulted, are not yet generally known at the grade for which the level has been prepared. The word list for Level Orange, for example, is comprised largely of words not known (again, according to the sources consulted) until at least fifth, sixth, or even seventh grade. From time to time, an exception has been made for a word on the basis of its appearance in standardized testing or in the curriculum at a specific grade.

The VOCABULARY WORKSHOP Program for Levels A-H

The Student Texts and Supplementary Testing Programs for Levels Orange and Blue are based on the same principles as, and are in many respects similar to, their counterparts at Levels A–H (grades 6–12+). There are some differences, however, in the number and types of components. Those for the program at Levels A–H are as follows:

- Student Texts, 8 Levels (A–H)
- Answer Keys, 8 Levels (A–H)
- Supplementary Testing Program
  - — Cycle One, 8 Levels (A–H)
  - — Cycle Two, 8 Levels (A–H)
  - — Combined Answer Keys, 8 Levels (A–H)
- SAT-Type TEST PREP Blackline Masters (answers included), 8 Levels (A–H)
- Interactive Audio Pronunciation Program, 6 Levels (A–F)
- Series Teacher's Guide, 1 volume

PROGRAM COMPONENTS FOR LEVEL Orange

Level Orange of VOCABULARY WORKSHOP consists of the following components:

- Student Text
- Supplementary Testing Program (Cycles One and Two)
- Teacher's Annotated Edition

The Student Text may be used alone or in conjunction with the Supplementary Testing Program. A suggested schedule for the year (based on 25 weeks) on pages xiv–xv provides an outline of how the Student Text and Supplementary Testing Program might be integrated.

THE STUDENT TEXT

Introductory Materials

The Vocabulary of Vocabulary

At the beginning of each Student Text there is a special section called *The Vocabulary of Vocabulary*. It has been provided to give students some useful concepts and terminology that they will apply throughout the VOCABULARY WORKSHOP program.

Many students will already be familiar with parts of speech and with synonyms and antonyms. The simple exercises that follow these two sections (see student pages 5 and 6) should be sufficient to clarify and consolidate this material.

The sections on Context Clues and Analogies (student pages 7 and 8) may require more time and attention, depending on the student's familiarity with these concepts and comfort with these skills.

The Diagnostic Test

After completing work on *The Vocabulary of Vocabulary,* it is advisable that the teacher assess the students' overall vocabulary and test-taking skills. The *Diagnostic Test* on student pages 10–11 has been provided for this purpose.

The Diagnostic Test allows for flexible use.

- It can be applied to give an *initial assessment* of the challenge that lies ahead.
- It also serves to give a *before-and-after comparison* when combined with the Final Mastery Test.

Although the Diagnostic Test may be presented as a timed speed test, with the specific aim of determining how many items students can answer in 10 to 15 minutes, it is better used as an informal motivational device. Speed will come when interest and mastery have been developed.

The Units

Having completed the preliminaries indicated above and made some assessment of the task ahead, the teacher is ready to take on the main work of the year, the study of the 192 key words presented in the 16 Units of each Student Text.

Structure of the Unit

The work of each Unit is divided into a unique *5-part structure* designed to give maximum coverage to each of the key words within the space available.

Definitions and Related Matters

1. Definitions The *definitions* provided are *not of the dictionary* type. They are, for the most part, relatively brief and simple. The intent is to give students a reasonably good "core" idea of what each word means, without extensive detail or secondary connotations.

Generally, only a single meaning of maximum usefulness is given. However, several meanings may be indicated if they are distinct or if they appear to be more or less equally useful.

- The **part of speech** of each word is indicated at the beginning of the definition, using a simple set of abbreviations. When a word functions as several parts of speech, the appropriate abbreviation appears before the corresponding definition.

- With each word listing, the **pronunciation** is indicated by means of a simple set of diacritical marks presented at the beginning of every Student Text (see student page 9).

The practice has been to indicate *only one pronunciation*, even where alternate pronunciations are sanctioned by the dictionary. There are only a few exceptions to this — mostly when a word changes its pronunciation in accordance with its use as different parts of speech.

- After each definition, the student is required to write the word in a blank space in an **illustrative sentence**. This offers no problem of selection, but it does focus attention on the illustrative sentence, and the act of writing is in itself a form of reinforcement. Also, writing out the word provides a good opportunity to focus attention on the spelling of the words.

It should be noted that the illustrative sentences provide a *context* that clarifies the meaning of each word and points out its idiomatic usage. By writing the word in such contextual settings, students begin to see how it can be used effectively in their own communication. In most cases, nouns appear in the singular and verbs in the present tense.

- The illustrative sentence is followed by a list of **synonyms** and **antonyms** (for those words that have either or both). The lists are not meant to be exhaustive, and care has been taken not to include legitimate but obscure synonyms or antonyms. The point of these lists is to familiarize the students with thesaurus clusters of which the target words are part.

2. Match the Meaning Following the definitions is a set of exercises designed to reinforce the students' understanding and recall of the meanings. In *Match the Meaning* the students must choose from four taught words (all of the same part of speech) the word indicated by the clue, which is usually formulated as an abridged version or paraphrase of the definition.

3. Synonyms and Antonyms In the *Synonyms and Antonyms* exercises students must select the taught word that is synonym (or antonym) to a highlighted word in an illustrative phrase. If an antonym, the highlighted word is one listed as such in the *Definitions* section; if a synonym, the word is either part of the definition or listed as a synonym in the *Definitions* section. Each of the 12 unit words is used once in either the *Synonyms* or *Antonyms*.

4. Completing the Sentence The next section is a completion exercise in which students are asked to choose and write the word from the unit that logically and meaningfully fits into a blank in a given sentence. Each word in a unit is used once. Students should be alerted to the fact that nouns may be used either in singular or plural, and that verbs may be used in any tense or form (participial, for example), as required by the sentence.

The items in this exercise are organized in groups, or clusters, of no fewer than three and no more than six, and are related by theme or subject matter. Most of the items consist of a single sentence, but a few extend to two. The clusters cover topics in history, geography, civics, science, and the arts, as well as many others of interest or relevance to the students.

Students are expected to use context clues within sentences or groups of sentences to choose the correct word for each item. (For more on context clues, see *The Vocabulary of Vocabulary,* page 5.) This exercise is designed in such a way as to give students practice both in using context as a guide to correct usage and word selection, and in developing test-taking strategies such as "process of elimination."

5. Word Associations The last section is a set of exercises challenging the students to *apply* what they have learned of the words in a way that calls for a measure of perception and imagination. It is expected that by this point the students will have absorbed the meanings and become familiar with the usage of the words. In *Word Associations* the students are asked to go one step further and demonstrate their knowledge by choosing the answer that best completes a sentence or answers a question highlighting the taught word.

Follow-up and Enrichment Activities

Cursive Practice
Students who require practice in cursive might copy the unit words in cursive handwriting on a separate sheet of paper or in a vocabulary journal.

Sentence Framing
Students who find it difficult to use unit words correctly might be given practice, either in class or as homework, in writing sentences of their own devising. These can be checked and corrected by the teacher or, if it seems advisable, by a peer.

Creative Writing
Most students enjoy writing. Accordingly, at the conclusion of work on a unit, students might be invited to create their own original stories or essays using a given number of key words they have just studied.

Unit Tests (Optional Purchase)
Once the work of the Unit in the Student Text has been completed, the teacher may administer the corresponding Unit Test in the Supplementary Testing Program (see p. xiii below).

The Reviews and Cumulative Reviews

A Review appears after each sequence of four Units, and covers only the words taught in those four units.

All four Reviews follow the same organization and feature the same sets of exercises, excepting the last set in each. **Word Games**, which concludes each review, differs from one to the next.

The Reviews begin with **Selecting Word Meanings**, which has the students match a taught word with a synonym or synonymous phrase. Next is **Spelling**. In this exercise students must first decide if a letter is missing from a taught word and, if one is missing, to supply it. Note that in no case is a word presented as deliberately misspelled. **Antonyms** is fashioned as in the units, with this difference: that in the Reviews the taught unit word, rather than a taught antonym, is given in the introductory phrase.

The two sections that follow, **Vocabulary in Context** and **Analogies**, have been included to provide further review and to give students practice in skills commonly assessed in standardized tests.

Vocabulary in Context is a cloze exercise that has students supply missing words in a passage. Although it is similar in some respects to **Completing the Sentence** (see p. x above), it differs in important ways: the passage flows uninterrupted, as in many standardized tests; it relies more on general context rather than restatement and contrast clues to point the students to the correct answers; and in format it approximates that found in many standardized tests.

The questions that conclude the exercise act as "tests" with which students can check their choices, and provide opportunities for the students themselves to use the words in sentences of their own devising.

The **Analogies** are valuable not merely as a kind of mental gymnastics but also as a means of pinning down the exact meanings of words and of correcting misconceptions or uncertainties about how those words are used. Analogies also provide an excellent means for cultivating and refining critical-thinking skills.

It is impossible, of course, to catalog all the relationships that may be embodied in analogy questions. They are as open-ended as the mental capacity to manipulate ideas and terms. The types of analogies found in the Reviews, however, have been kept to a number and to a degree of difficulty thought to be manageable by students at grades 4-6. Most of the analogies are of a purely vocabulary-based nature; that is, the relationship between the key words is either that of synonyms or antonyms.

Each of the **Analogies** exercises concludes with a "Challenge" item asking students to write a comparison based on given words. All of the analogies that may be made from the words, as well as explanations of the relationships, can be found on p. xxiv of this Guide.

The **Word Families** section has been designed to help students expand and enrich their vocabularies by building upon the words presented in the units.

Word Games, which concludes the Review, presents a final reinforcement of usage and meaning in the form of a game or puzzle.

Cumulative Reviews

Two Cumulative Reviews have been provided in the Student Text, one following the Review for Units 5–8 and one following the Review for Units 13–16. Cumulative Review I covers the words presented in the first half of the book (Units 1–8), and Cumulative Review II covers the words presented in the second half (Units 9–16).

The sets of exercises included in the Cumulative Reviews are straightforward in nature, and in format have been designed in such a way as to maximize the number of words to be reviewed. In the **Definitions** and **Antonyms** sections students must match definitions and antonyms to taught words. **Completing the Sentence** is similar in purpose to the corresponding exercise in the Units, but in the Cumulative Reviews students are given a limited number of words from which to choose, and the sentences are not thematically related.

The **Classifying** exercise is unique to the Cumulative Reviews. This exercise challenges the students to look at the taught words from new and interesting perspectives, to recognize relationships between words, and to see as well that these words may be considered as members of larger classes or categories of vocabulary.

Follow-up and Enrichment Activities

Phonics
Teachers may find it opportune to help students with instruction in (or review of) phonics skills in conjunction with the *Spelling* exercise. Some students may find it difficult to isolate sounds in multisyllabic words.

Affixes
Teachers may wish to build on the *Word Families* exercise to have the students identify and discuss prefixes, suffixes, and common word endings found among the words under review.

Mastery Tests (Optional Purchase)
Once the work of the Review in the Student Text has been completed, the teacher may administer the corresponding *Mastery Test* in Cycle One or Two of the Supplementary Testing Program (see p. xiii below).

Final Mastery Test

The **Final Mastery Test** in the Student Text (student pages 140–143) is designed as a practice test of 50 items that gives students and teachers reasonably good insight into how much progress has been made during the year and what kind of additional work is in order.

The exercise types are for the most part the same as or similar to those in the Units and Reviews. The exception is **Part of Speech**, which occurs only in the Final Mastery Test. In this exercise students must identify the part of speech of a taught word as it is used in an illustrative phrase.

The purpose of the Final Mastery Test is threefold.

- It can serve as an informal evaluation of achievement to date;
- It can serve as a reinforcement activity;
- It can serve as a before-and-after comparison when used in conjunction with the Diagnostic Test.

For whichever purpose the test is used, it is both *a testing and a teaching device*, the culminating step in a process involving many class periods and therefore should be given careful attention.

SUPPLEMENTARY TESTING PROGRAM
(Optional Purchase)

The *Supplementary Testing Program* for Level Orange consists of two student Test Booklets (designated Cycle One and Cycle Two) designed to be used for varied and secure testing over a two-year period. It may be used purely as a testing program following the completion of work on the corresponding part or parts of the Student Text. Or it may be used for reteaching purposes. Or it may be tailored to serve some combination of purposes, depending upon the progress and achievement of a class or of individual students. The yearly and weekly plans given on pages xiv–xvii outline ways in which the Student Text and the Supplementary Testing Program might be used together to best advantage.

The Test Booklets are organized to mirror closely that of the Student Text. A 2-page Unit Test is provided for each of the 16 Units, a 2-page Mastery Test to correspond with each of the four Reviews, and a 4-page Final Mastery Test to supplement that in the Student Text. (There are no Cumulative Reviews in the Supplementary Testing Program.)

The Unit Test consists of 25 items; and the four sets of exercises in each (**Match the Meaning**, **Completing the Sentence**, **Synonyms**, and **Antonyms**) follow their counterparts in the Units and Reviews of the Student Text.

The Mastery Test is comprised of four sets of exercises as well. In **Word Meanings** students must match definitions with given words. The **Part of Speech** exercise is identical to that found in the Final Mastery Test of the Student Text. And in format and design the two sets of items in **Completing the Sentence** follow that of the Cumulative Reviews found in the Student Text.

In the Final Mastery Test are 50 consecutively numbered items, again including **Word Meanings**, **Completing the Sentence**, **Synonyms**, and **Antonyms**. Also included in the Final Mastery Test are a **Spelling** exercise and a **Word Associations** exercise patterned after those in the Student Text.

The answers to all of the items tested in the Supplementary Testing Program are given in the keys on pages xxv–xxxii of this Guide.

IMPLEMENTING THE PROGRAM

The format of the VOCABULARY WORKSHOP program allows for great flexibility. The teacher can easily adjust the activity assignments to conform to the special needs of an entire class, of groups within the class, or of individual students.

Schedule for the Year (25 Weeks)

The chart below shows how the various components of the VOCABULARY WORKSHOP program can be scheduled effectively over an academic year lasting 25 weeks. (The abbreviation STP C1/C2 stands for Supplementary Testing Program Cycle One or Two.)

Week	Student Text	Follow-Up Activities
1	Vocabulary of Vocabulary	
2	Diagnostic Test	
3	Unit 1	Creative Writing Unit Test 1 (STP C1/C2)
4	Unit 2	Creative Writing Unit Test 2 (STP C1/C2)
5	Unit 3	Creative Writing Unit Test 3 (STP C1/C2)
6	Unit 4	Creative Writing Unit Test 4 (STP C1/C2)
7	Review Units 1–4	Reviewing Phonics Mastery Test 1 (STP C1/C2)
8	Unit 5	Unit Test 5 (STP C1/C2) Creative Writing
9	Unit 6	Unit Test 6 (STP C1/C2) Creative Writing
10	Unit 7	Unit Test 7 (STP C1/C2) Creative Writing
11	Unit 8	Unit Test 8 (STP C1/C2) Creative Writing
12	Review Units 5–8	Mastery Test 2 (STP C1/C2) Reviewing Phonics
13	Cumulative Test 1–8	
14	Unit 9	Unit Test 9 (STP C1/C2) Creative Writing

Week	Student Text	Follow-Up Activities
15	Unit 10	Unit Test 10 (STP C1/C2) Creative Writing
16	Unit 11	Unit Test 11 (STP C1/C2) Creative Writing
17	Unit 12	Unit Test 12 (STP C1/C2) Creative Writing
18	Review Units 9–12	Mastery Test 3 (STP C1/C2) Reviewing Phonics
19	Unit 13	Unit Test 13 (STP C1/C2) Creative Writing
20	Unit 14	Unit Test 14 (STP C1/C2) Creative Writing
21	Unit 15	Unit Test 15 (STP C1/C2) Creative Writing
22	Unit 16	Unit Test 16 (STP C1/C2) Creative Writing
23	Review Units 13–16	Mastery Test 4 (STP C1/C2) Reviewing Phonics
24	Cumulative Review 9–16	Final Mastery Test (STP C1/C2)
25	Final Mastery Test	

The following notes should prove helpful when adapting the chart to individual needs:

• Though the chart shows a disposition of material over 25 weeks, the time period can be extended to as many as 31 weeks simply by increasing the time allotment for the items under weeks 7, 12, 18, 23, 24, and 25, to 2 weeks.

• It is *not* to be supposed that *every* item listed under Follow-Up Activities is meant to be covered during the week specified. The listings here are designed to offer teacher options from which to choose in order to tailor the VOCABULARY WORKSHOP program to the specific needs of a particular class. This is also true of the sections or subsections into which some of the Follow-Up components are divided.

• The average time allotment per class session is estimated to be about 20 minutes, but here again teachers will have to adapt this estimate to the needs of individual groups.

Weekly Schedules

There is no single formula or plan that will be sure to yield optimum results for the program. Experience will soon guide the teacher to modifications that are likely to work best under specific conditions.

Using the Units

Following are two plans for using the Units effectively on a weekly basis:

Weekly Plan for Using the Units

MODEL A — 3 Sessions (35–40 minutes)		
Day	Classwork	Homework
1	Present Definitions Present Pronunciation Write each word	Match the Meaning Synonyms/Antonyms
2	Completing the Sentence Word Associations	Correct previous homework Write sentences Test study
3	Unit Test (STP C1/C2)	Review corrected sentences

MODEL B — 5 Sessions (20 minutes)		
Day	Classwork	Homework
1	Present Definitions Present Pronunciation Review Unit Test	Match the Meaning Add illustrative sentences to Vocabulary Notebook
2	Review Match the Meaning Write each word	Synonyms/Antonyms
3	Review Synonyms/Antonyms Completing the Sentence	Word Associations Write sentences
4	Review Word Associations Review sentences	Test study
5	Unit Test (STP C1/C2)	Review corrected sentences

Using the Reviews

Following are two models for using the Reviews effectively on a weekly basis.

Weekly Plan for using the Reviews

MODEL A — 3 Sessions (35–40 minutes)		
Day	Classwork	Homework
1	Present: Selecting Word Meanings Spelling/Phonics* Antonyms Word Associations	Vocabulary in Context Analogies Phonics assignment*
2	Review homework Word Families Word Games Review phonics*	Test study
3	Mastery Test (STP C1/C2)	Remedial work as needed

MODEL B — 5 Sessions (20 minutes)		
Day	Classwork	Homework
1	Selecting Word Meanings Analogies	Spelling Word Families
2	Review Spelling/Phonics* Review Word Families	Antonyms Vocabulary in Context
3	Review Antonyms Review Vocabulary in Context	Word Games
4	Share Analogies Parts of Speech	Test study
5	Mastery Test (STP C1/C2)	

*See p. xii for reference to phonics skills

Using the Cumulative Reviews

Following are two models for using the Cumulative Reviews effectively on a weekly basis.

Weekly Plan for Using the Cumulative Reviews

MODEL A — 3 Sessions (35–40 minutes)		
Day	**Classwork**	**Homework**
1	Definitions Antonyms	Completing the Sentence
2	Review Completing the Sentence Classifying	Test study
3	Remediate as needed	

MODEL B — 5 Sessions (20 minutes)		
1	Definitions	Antonyms
2	Review Antonyms	Completing the Sentence
3	Review Completing the Sentence	Classifying
4	Review Classifying	Test study
5	Remediate as needed	

Implementing the Weekly Schedules

The following may prove helpful when adapting the foregoing schedules to specific situations.

• The models shown are, as their designation suggests, *purely models*—that is, starting points. Accordingly, the teacher is expected to adapt them to the particular situation at hand.

• Place assignments and timings are to some extent hypothetical. Teachers should switch items around and adjust timings as needed. Similarly, items may be modified or deleted and new items inserted as the teacher sees fit.

• Multiple listings in a Day's entry for either Classwork or Homework are to be seen as options from which the teacher should select appropriate material. It is unlikely that the teacher could cover all the suggested material in the indicated time allotment.

• With some adjustment, the allotments for each day can accommodate a 2- or 4-day arrangement. There is usually too much material to cover in 1 day, and a 1-day approach is, therefore, *not* suggested.

Alternative Approaches to Using the Program

Writing Approach

Research has shown that vocabulary acquisition is maximized when learning is authentically contextualized—when learners have a "real-life" purpose for acquiring and using a new word. Activities such as the following can provide these authentic contexts.

• Students can create *Vocabulary Journals* in which they use the key words to express experiences, thoughts, or feelings that are personally meaningful. They are free to keep these entries for their eyes only or to share them with others.

• Students can use the key words in personal letters to friends and relatives or in letters to the editor of the school or local newspaper. Students should write about subjects of real interest and concern to them.

• Students can use the key words to write descriptions of people they know or characters they are interested in. These character sketches or personality profiles may be written for a class yearbook, for a book report, or as a reference for a friend.

Literature-Based Approach

The VOCABULARY WORKSHOP program for Levels Orange and Blue can be combined with the titles listed below to form a *literature-based approach* to vocabulary study. Seeing the words they are studying in action in classic and contemporary literature will reinforce student appreciation of the value of possessing a good active-use vocabulary.

Literature to Use with the Program		
Author	**Title**	**Type**
Avi	*Poppy*	Animal/Adventure
Babbit, Natalie	*The Search for Delicious*	Fantasy/Dictionary Definitions
Banks, Lynne Reid	*The Indian in the Cupboard*	Fantasy/Adventure
Brink, Carol Ryrie	*Caddie Woodlawn*	Historical/Prairie
Brittain, Bill	*The Wish Giver*	Mystery/Suspense
Burnford, Shirley	*The Incredible Journey*	Animal/Adventure
Byars, Betsy	*Summer of the Swans*	Realistic/Family
Clement, Andrew	*Frindle*	Realistic/History of Language
Conrad, Pam	*My Daniel* *Our House*	Mystery/Historical Prairie Short Stories/Humor/Levittown
Curtis, Christopher Paul	*The Watsons Go to Birmingham–1963*	Historical/African American
Dorris, Michael	*Morning Girl*	Historical/Native American
Fitzgerald, John D.	*The Great Brain*	Realistic/Humor
Fitzhugh, Louise	*Harriet the Spy*	Realistic/Humor
Fleischman, Sid	*The Whipping Boy*	Fantasy/Adventure
Gardiner, John R.	*Stone Fox*	Adventure/Historical
George, Jean Craighead	*My Side of the Mountain*	Adventure/Survival

Author	Title	Type
Gipson, Frederick	*Old Yeller*	Animal/Realistic
Gray, Lulu	*Falcon's Egg*	Fantasy/Family
King-Smith, Dick	*Babe: The Gallant Pig*	Animal/Humor
	School Mouse	Animal/Books & Reading
Konigsburg, E.L.	*The View From Saturday*	Realistic/Language Contest
Lawson, Robert	*Ben and Me*	Historical/Franklin/Animal
Lofting, Hugh	*The Story of Doctor Doolittle*	Animal/Fantasy/Adventure
Lord, Betty Bao	*In the Year of the Boar and Jackie Robinson*	Historical/Chinese-American
Lowry, Lois	*Number the Stars*	Historical/WWII
MacLachlan, Patricia	*Sarah Plain and Tall*	Historical/Prairie
	The Facts and Fictions of Minna Pratt	Realistic/Musicians
McCloskey, Robert	*Homer Price*	Short Stories/Humor
Merrill, Jean	*The Pushcart War*	Realistic/Humor
Mohr, Nicholasa	*Felita*	Realistic/Hispanic
Mowat, Farley	*Owls in the Family*	Autobiography
Naylor, Phyllis Reynolds	*Shiloh*	Realistic/Animal
Noble, Sarah	*The Courage of Sarah Noble*	Autobiography/Westward Expansion
North, Sterling	*Rascal*	Autobiography/Animal/Humor
Norton, Mary	*The Borrowers*	Fantasy/Family
O'Brien, Robert	*Mrs. Frisby and the Rats of Nimh*	Animal/Fantasy
Paulson, Gary	*Hatchet*	Adventure/Survival
Sebestyn, Ouida	*Words by Heart*	Historical/African-American/Bible Studies
Snyder, Zilpha Keatley	*Cat Running*	Historical/Great Depression/Dust Bowl
Spinelli, Jerry	*Maniac Magee*	Realistic/Tall Tale
Steig, William	*Dominic*	Animal/Humor/Fantasy
Tate, Eleanor	*Thank You, Dr. Martin Luther King Jr.*	Historical/Realistic
Taylor, Mildred	*Mississippi Bridge*	Historical/African-American/Prejudice
Taylor, Sidney	*All-of-a-Kind Family*	Historical Fiction/NYC/Jewish
Woodson, Jacqueline	*Last Summer with Maizon*	African-American/Friendship/Realistic
Yep, Lawrence	*Dragonwings*	Historical/San Francisco Earthquake/Chinese-American

To coordinate reading and vocabulary study, the following may prove helpful:

• Suggest to the students that they copy into their Vocabulary Journals the taught words that they come across in their reading, and that they copy out, too, the sentence in which the word has been used, the author's name, and the title of the work.

Content-Area Approach

VOCABULARY WORKSHOP can be used to enhance student understanding and use of vocabulary in other areas of the curriculum such as social studies and history, science and health, consumer education and economics, by making use of the following strategies:

• Students, working in pairs or small groups, can choose sentence clusters from *Completing the Sentence* or *Vocabulary in Context* and discuss the larger context in which these sentences could have appeared, such as in a history or mathematics textbook, a daily newspaper, a book review, a personal letter, or a scientific article.

• Students can work together to link individual vocabulary words to a *particular content area*. Then working in pairs, they can find "real-world" examples of the words used in context in that content area.

Useful Classroom Techniques

Classroom experience and research have shown that some students learn more readily when they can exercise a great deal of personal choice and interact with others. VOCABULARY WORKSHOP can be adapted in the following ways to accommodate such students.

Cooperative Activities

Working cooperatively does not just mean working in proximity to other students or dividing an assignment or project into discrete tasks. Rather it means that students take individual and collective responsibility for the learning of all members of the group and for the successful completion of the group goal.

Oral and Kinesthetic Activities

• One student can write the taught words in a given Unit on the chalkboard while the rest of the class is divided into pairs or small groups. A member of each group will read a numbered item from the Unit aloud. The rest of the group will confer and then supply the required vocabulary word.

• Students can work together to create puns, riddles and rhymes using the words. They may want to collect and publish their creations in illustrated books.

• Members of a group can work together to improvise stories, skits, or pantomimes that illustrate the meanings of the words in a given Unit, while other group members guess the word being illustrated.

Written Activities

• Students can work together in pairs or small groups to create their own vocabulary lists, based on their reading in all areas of the curriculum and on their personal reading and writing.

• The class might as a whole make up a unit of their own, based upon the structure of the units in the Student Text. Students might be assigned to work in groups to develop each part of the unit.

• Students might create their own mini-dictionaries based on the word lists in VOCABULARY WORKSHOP and/or on categories or groups of words that are of particular importance or meaning to them.

Alternative Types of Assessment

The following types of assessment may be used in addition to or in lieu of the objective-scoring materials provided in the VOCABULARY WORKSHOP. The emphasis here is on monitoring understanding rather than on ranking students.

Self-Evaluation

Students can use their journals to reflect on their own process of learning and use of new words. They may consider, for example, which words from Level Orange of VOCABULARY WORKSHOP they understood quickly and used frequently and why.

Teacher-Student Conferencing

Meetings take place at every stage of the vocabulary-acquisition process. Meeting over time allows teachers to assess students' developing understanding of words as used in specific contexts.

Observation

Using a checklist of two or three important criteria, the teacher can observe and evaluate students while they are interacting in groups or engaging in other oral activities. Teachers can also probe for deeper levels of comprehension by asking students to clarify or give reasons for their choice of word or context.

Peer Evaluation

Students meet in pairs or small groups to develop standards to evaluate their vocabulary. They then apply their standards to their peers' oral or written expression, giving positive feedback and concrete suggestions for improvement.

Portfolio Assessment

By having students collect and save self-selected samples of their writing over a period of time, teachers have an ongoing record of students' vocabulary development and of their facility in using words in context.

Multimodal Assessment

Students with strong nonverbal competencies can be given the opportunity to demonstrate in nonverbal media their understanding of new vocabulary. For example, they can draw, paint, model, dance, compose music, or construct objects to communicate their comprehension of a word and its definition.

Teacher Resources

The following lists have been compiled to assist the teacher in the effective presentation of the VOCABULARY WORKSHOP program.

Dictionaries

Merriam Webster *Collegiate Dictionary* [Tenth Edition] (Springfield, MA: Merriam Webster, 1994)

Webster's Third New International Dictionary (Springfield, MA: G. & C. Merriam, 1971)

12,000 Words [A Supplement to Webster's *Third International Dictionary*] (Springfield, MA: Merriam Webster, 1986)

American Heritage Dictionary (Boston: Houghton Mifflin, 1982)

The Random House Dictionary of the English Language [Unabridged Edition] (NY: Random House, 1987)

Thesauri

Roget's II The New Thesaurus (Boston: Houghton Mifflin, 1988)

Chapman, R.L. (Ed.). *Roget A to Z* (NY: Harper Perennial, 1994)

Laird, C. *Webster's New World Thesaurus* (NY: Warner Books, 1990)

Random House Thesaurus (NY: Random House, 1984)

Rodale, J. [Revised by Urdang, L. and La Roche, N.] *The Synonym Finder* (Emmaus, PA: Rodale Press, 1978)

Urdang, L. *The Oxford Thesaurus* (NY: Oxford University Press, 1992)

Other Useful Resources

Bernstein, T. *Reverse Dictionary* (NY: Random House, 1988)

Bryson, B. *A Dictionary of Troublesome Words* (NY: Viking Penguin, 1988)

DeVries, M. *The Complete Word Book* (Englewood Cliffs, NJ: Prentice-Hall, 1991)

Dixson, R. *Essential Idioms in English* (Englewood Cliffs, NJ: Prentice ESL, 1987)

Evans, I. H. (Ed.) *Brewer's Dictionary of Phrase & Fable* (NY: Harper & Row, 1981)

Harrison, G. *Vocabulary Dynamics* (NY: Warner Books, 1992)

Lemay, H. et al. *The Facts on File Dictionary of New Words* (NY: Facts on File, 1989)

Morris, W. and M. Morris *Dictionary of Word & Phrase Origins* (NY: Harper & Row, 1981)

Orgel, J.R. *Building an Enriched Vocabulary* (NY: William H. Sadlier, Inc., 1995)

Paxson, W. *New American Dictionary of Confusing Words* (NY: NAL-Dutton, 1990)

Shipley, J. *Dictionary of Word Origins* (Glenville, IL: Greenwood Press, 1988)

Webster's Word Histories (Springfield, MA: Merriam Webster, 1989)

Computer Resources

GENERAL REFERENCE

American Heritage Electronic Dictionary III WordStar

Encarta: A Multimedia Encyclopedia Microsoft

WORD STUDY

Analogies Tutorial Hartley Courseware

IBM Vocabulary Series Level IV IBM Educational Systems

Lucky 7 Vocabulary Games—Intermediate Que

Testtaker's Edge with Words Que

Vocabulary Building II Resource Software

Vocabulary Building Skills IBM Educational Systems

Vocabulary Source Files—Junior High Microphys Programs

Word Knowledge Skills IBM Educational Systems

Answers to Challenge Exercises in Analogies Section of Reviews:

Review I, p. 39

Analogy: **rung** is to **ladder** as **step** is to **stair**
Relationship: A rung is part of a ladder; a step is part of a stair.

Analogy: **tuna** is to **fish** as **robin** is to **bird**
Relationship: A tuna is a kind of fish; a robin is a kind of bird.

Analogy: **burden** is to **hardship** as **basic** is to **essential**
Relationship: *Burden* means the same as *hardship*; *basic* means the same as *essential*. *Burden* and *hardship* are synonyms; *basic* and *essential* are synonyms.

Review II, p. 69

Analogy: **petal** is to **flower** as **page** is to **book**
Relationship: A petal is part of a flower; a page is part of a book.

Analogy: **scholar** is to **study** as **pioneer** is to **explore**
Relationship: A scholar is someone who studies; a pioneer is someone who explores.

Analogy: **triumph** is to **joy** as **disaster** is to **grief**
Relationship: A triumph would bring joy; a disaster would bring grief.

Review III, p. 103

Analogy: **camera** is to **lens** as **computer** is to **screen**
Relationship: A camera has a lens; a computer has a screen.

Analogy: **chair** is to **furniture** as **car** is to **vehicle**
Relationship: A chair is a kind of furniture; a car is a kind of vehicle.

Analogy: **toxic** is to **safe** as **shrink** is to **magnify**
Relationship: *Toxic* is opposite in meaning to *safe*; *shrink* is opposite in meaning to *magnify*. *Toxic* and *safe* are antonyms; *shrink* and *magnify* are antonyms.

Review IV, p. 133

Analogy: **sand** is to **beach** as **grass** is to **lawn**
Relationship: Sand is found on a beach; grass is found on a lawn.

Analogy: **red** is to **color** as **triangle** is to **shape**
Relationship: Red is a color; triangle is a shape.

Analogy: **tiny** is to **colossal** as **ally** is to **enemy**
Relationship: *Tiny* is opposite in meaning to *colossal*; *ally* is opposite in meaning to *enemy*. *Tiny* and *colossal* are antonyms; *ally* and *enemy* are antonyms.

Answer Key to Level Orange Supplementary Testing Program
Cycle One

UNIT 1
1. **b** celebrity
2. **d** demonstrate
3. **c** hardship
4. **a** haul
5. **a** humble
6. **d** pledge
7. **b** suitable
8. counsel
9. drowsy
10. essential
11. sincere
12. stampede
13. demonstrate
14. **b** rush
15. **d** promise
16. **b** catch
17. **a** difficulty
18. **d** advise
19. **c** show
20. **c** nobody
21. **a** alert
22. **d** unnecessary
23. **b** grand
24. **a** phony
25. **c** inappropriate

UNIT 2
1. **c** vacant
2. **a** portion
3. **b** obtain
4. **d** dismiss
5. **d** basics
6. **c** competition
7. **a** neglect
8. annual
9. contract
10. neglect
11. recall
12. sponsor
13. stern
14. **b** yearbook
15. **d** fundamental
16. **a** helping
17. **c** memory
18. **b** supporters
19. **d** sharp
20. **a** cooperation
21. **d** expand
22. **c** hold
23. **b** pamper
24. **c** lose
25. **a** occupied

UNIT 3
1. **d** Attractive
2. **a** consent
3. **c** indicate
4. **b** qualify
5. **c** dependable
6. **a** burden
7. **d** response
8. previous
9. shabby
10. thawed
11. vanity
12. response
13. urgent
14. **b** load
15. **c** authorization
16. **a** reaction
17. **d** conceit
18. **b** melt
19. **c** prepare
20. **b** unreliable
21. **a** conceal
22. **c** following
23. **c** kind
24. **a** unimportant
25. **d** unappealing

UNIT 4
1. **b** ambush
2. **d** contribute
3. **a** employs
4. **c** routine
5. **c** sturdy
6. **b** initials
7. **a** Frantic
8. calculate
9. dread
10. extend
11. stunned
12. routine
13. yields
14. **d** surrender to
15. **c** attack
16. **a** desperate
17. **d** hire
18. **b** astonish
19. **c** evaluate
20. **a** welcome
21. **d** final
22. **c** delicate
23. **a** withhold
24. **b** decrease
25. **b** unusual

MASTERY TEST I (UNITS 1–4)
1. urgent
2. sincere
3. dread
4. recall
5. extend
6. V
7. N
8. A
9. A
10. V
11. V
12. N
13. V
14. N
15. A
16. pledge
17. vacant
18. qualify
19. stampede
20. essential
21. suitable
22. burden
23. ambush
24. response
25. employ

UNIT 5
1. **a** baggage
2. **c** haste
3. **b** oppose
4. **d** humid
5. **c** worthy
6. **b** establish
7. **a** antiques
8. digest

Cycle One

9. lashed
10. sensible
11. antique
12. pioneers
13. eternal
14. **d** eat
15. **d** protest
16. **b** deserving of
17. **a** a hurry
18. **c** originate
19. **b** luggage
20. **a** fleeting
21. **d** modern
22. **c** dry
23. **b** foolish
24. **d** destroy
25. **c** untie

UNIT 6

1. **a** blossom
2. **d** drought
3. **c** noble
4. **b** constant
5. **d** quiver
6. **b** collide
7. **c** slight
8. Foul
9. content
10. tidy
11. policy
12. distract
13. collide
14. **a** continuous
15. **a** guidelines
16. **c** minor
17. **b** grows
18. **d** tremble
19. **c** good
20. **b** unhappy
21. **a** flood
22. **d** tiny
23. **c** focus
24. **d** cleanse
25. **b** agree

UNIT 7

1. **d** disasters
2. **b** accurate
3. **a** feeble

4. **c** envy
5. **b** romp
6. **d** staple
7. **a** alert
8. penetrate
9. survive
10. ancestors
11. epidemic
12. elementary
13. feeble
14. **c** infection
15. **a** forebears
16. **d** frolic
17. **c** begrudge
18. **b** pierce
19. **d** warning
20. **a** success
21. **c** forceful
22. **c** nonessentials
23. **b** advanced
24. **d** perish
25. **c** false

UNIT 8

1. **a** awkward
2. **b** plentiful
3. **a** scholar
4. **d** ration
5. **c** clatter
6. **b** lukewarm
7. **d** gallant
8. weary
9. reserve
10. awkward
11. volunteer
12. plentiful
13. trudged
14. **c** share
15. **a** offer
16. **d** authority
17. **c** rattle
18. **b** slog
19. **b** caution
20. **a** slob
21. **c** scarce
22. **d** graceful
23. **b** energized by
24. **d** explode
25. **c** enthusiastic

MASTERY TEST II (UNITS 5–8)

1. establish
2. trudge
3. ancestor
4. feeble
5. policy
6. V   11. V
7. N   12. N
8. A   13. V
9. A   14. N
10. V   15. A
16. lash
17. tidy
18. disaster
19. clatter
20. collide
21. pioneer
22. content
23. staple
24. lukewarm
25. noble

UNIT 9

1. **c** disciplines
2. **c** enclose
3. **a** uneasy
4. **d** treaty
5. **b** grumble
6. **a** convict
7. **d** earnest
8. dungeon
9. nourish
10. jagged
11. discipline
12. gradual
13. provision
14. **b** rugged
15. **c** cell
16. **d** preparations
17. **a** sustain
18. **d** pact
19. **b** complain
20. **c** release
21. **b** foolish
22. **d** sudden
23. **a** certain
24. **c** omit
25. **b** disorder

Cycle One

UNIT 10

1. **c** outstanding
2. **a** tardy
3. **d** dwell
4. **b** register
5. **a** juvenile
6. **d** distress
7. **b** drench
8. sift
9. distress
10. unfit
11. spree
12. variety
13. proceed
14. **c** unsuitable
15. **b** filter
16. **a** reside
17. **d** splurge
18. **c** douse
19. **d** express
20. **b** mature
21. **a** retreat
22. **c** early
23. **b** ordinary
24. **d** sameness
25. **a** soothe

UNIT 11

1. **d** elevate
2. **c** missionaries
3. **b** site
4. **a** extraordinary
5. **b** blockade
6. **c** pointless
7. **d** despair
8. herioc
9. chants
10. toxic
11. reflect
12. despair
13. lanced
14. **a** location
15. **d** preacher
16. **b** promote
17. **c** intone
18. **c** remarkable
19. **b** spear
20. **d** open
21. **a** effective

22. **c** harmless
23. **a** hope
24. **d** retain
25. **b** cowardly

UNIT 12

1. **b** coarse
2. **a** focus
3. **c** circulars
4. **d** quake
5. **d** bristle
6. **a** discard
7. **c** grasp
8. inspired
9. focus
10. marine
11. troublesome
12. magnify
13. extreme
14. **b** enlarge
15. **b** seethe
16. **c** tremor
17. **d** ring-shaped
18. **a** hard
19. **d** oceanic
20. **b** smooth
21. **d** misunderstand
22. **a** usual
23. **c** discouraged
24. **a** save
25. **b** background

MASTERY TEST III (UNITS 9–12)

1. lance
2. convict
3. jagged
4. drench
5. troublesome
6. V   11. V
7. N   12. N
8. A   13. V
9. A   14. N
10. V   15. A
16. earnest
17. spree
18. chant
19. magnify
20. elevate

21. enclose
22. dwell
23. grasp
24. extreme
25. register

UNIT 13

1. **b** noticeable
2. **d** appoint
3. **c** courtesy
4. **a** attentive
5. **a** overthrow
6. **b** bonus
7. **d** carefree
8. peculiar
9. abstract
10. mistrust
11. attentive
12. ally
13. manufactured
14. **c** concoct
15. **a** theoretical
16. **a** unique
17. **b** defeat
18. **d** doubt
19. **d** partner
20. **c** fine
21. **a** disregard
22. **b** inconsiderate
23. **a** anxious
24. **b** hidden
25. **c** dismiss

UNIT 14

1. **a** hazardous
2. **c** necessity
3. **b** deliberate
4. **d** regain
5. **c** thorough
6. **d** huddle
7. **a** absolute
8. compliment
9. dominant
10. offend
11. dense
12. arena
13. deliberate
14. **b** stadium
15. **a** cluster

Cycle One

16. **b** complete
17. **d** recovered
18. **c** praise
19. **a** exhaustive
20. **b** careless
21. **c** secondary
22. **d** safe
23. **b** please
24. **a** luxury
25. **c** thin

UNIT 15

1. **c** assist
2. **a** merit
3. **b** genuine
4. **d** babble
5. **c** illegal
6. **d** fatal
7. **a** adopt
8. drab
9. generosity
10. agile
11. illegal
12. captivity
13. analyze
14. **b** jabber
15. **a** help
16. **b** prohibited
17. **d** deadly
18. **c** excellence
19. **c** examine
20. **b** freedom
21. **d** clumsy
22. **a** greed
23. **b** desert
24. **d** fake
25. **a** cheerful

UNIT 16

1. **d** assemble
2. **a** frail
3. **a** warrants
4. **b** landslide
5. **c** adorn
6. **d** rampage
7. **b** effective
8. colossal
9. symptoms
10. scamper

11. assemble
12. appropriate
13. hostage
14. **a** avalanche
15. **c** prisoners
16. **b** justify
17. **a** indications
18. **a** raged
19. **c** decorate
20. **b** separate
21. **d** useless
22. **b** healthy
23. **d** unsuitable
24. **a** stroll
25. **c** small

MASTERY TEST IV (UNITS 13–16)

1. deliberate
2. adorn
3. babble
4. hostage
5. abstract
6. V
7. N
8. A
9. A
10. V
11. V
12. N
13. V
14. N
15. A
16. attentive
17. huddle
18. merit
19. regain
20. agile
21. carefree
22. thorough
23. fatal
24. appropriate
25. frail

FINAL MASTERY TEST

1. humble
2. vanity
3. penetrate
4. smolder
5. outstanding
6. despair
7. circular
8. arena
9. genuine

10. scamper
11. yield
12. slight
13. counsel
14. plentiful
15. treaty
16. extraordinary
17. stern
18. quake
19. necessity
20. adopt
21. grumble
22. weary
23. sift
24. mistrust
25. compliment
26. juvenile
27. discard
28. reflect
29. **c** get
30. **a** bewilder
31. **d** deserving
32. **b** jealousy
33. **b** grainy
34. **a** charity
35. **d** lose
36. **c** caution
37. **d** relaxed
38. **a** harmless
39. **c** common
40. **b** weak
41. **a**
42. **c**
43. **b**
44. **d**
45. **b**
46. **c**
47. **d**
48. **d**
49. **c**
50. **b**

Answer Key to Level Orange Supplementary Testing Program Cycle Two

UNIT 1

1. **d** hardship
2. **a** essential
3. **c** demonstrate
4. **b** celebrity
5. **b** stampede
6. **d** drowsy
7. **c** counsel
8. pledge
9. suitable
10. haul
11. drowsy
12. humble
13. sincere
14. **a** essential
15. **d** advise
16. **b** carry
17. **c** swear
18. **c** misfortune
19. **a** prove
20. **b** grand
21. **a** phony
22. **d** inappropriate
23. **c** stroll
24. **a** alert
25. **d** nobody

UNIT 2

1. **b** basic
2. **c** contract
3. **d** stern
4. **a** annual
5. **d** recall
6. **b** sponsor
7. **c** portion
8. contract
9. obtain
10. vacant
11. neglect
12. dismiss
13. competition
14. **a** drop
15. **c** essential
16. **b** empty
17. **d** support
18. **d** acquire
19. **a** yearly
20. **c** whole
21. **a** expand
22. **b** kindly
23. **d** pamper
24. **b** cooperation
25. **a** forget

UNIT 3

1. **a** Vanity
2. **d** previous
3. **b** urgent
4. **b** response
5. **c** thaw
6. **c** shabby
7. **a** indicate
8. burden
9. dependable
10. indicate
11. attractive
12. qualify
13. consent
14. **d** answer
15. **c** responsible
16. **a** earlier
17. **b** beautiful
18. **a** signify
19. **b** prepare
20. **c** modesty
21. **d** relieve
22. **b** elegant
23. **a** unimportant
24. **d** freeze
25. **c** refuse

UNIT 4

1. **c** yield
2. **b** calculate
3. **a** extend
4. **d** routine
5. **b** contribute
6. **a** stun
7. **d** dread
8. frantic
9. employs
10. sturdy
11. contributes
12. initial
13. ambush
14. **c** figure
15. **b** astonish
16. **d** continue
17. **a** waylay
18. **c** terror
19. **c** donate
20. **b** resist
21. **a** dismiss
22. **d** unusual
23. **c** calm
24. **a** weak
25. **b** final

MASTERY TEST I (UNITS 1–4)

1. obtain
2. stun
3. counsel
4. routine
5. neglect
6. V
7. A
8. N
9. A
10. V
11. A
12. N
13. A
14. A
15. V
16. previous
17. basic
18. calculate
19. haul
20. thaw
21. hardship
22. yield
23. vanity
24. annual
25. urgent

Cycle Two

UNIT 5

1. **d** sensible
2. **a** digest
3. **c** lash
4. **c** antique
5. **a** eternal
6. **d** pioneer
7. **b** haste
8. haste
9. baggage
10. opposed
11. worthy
12. establish
13. humid
14. **b** prove
15. **a** tie
16. **d** trunks
17. **c** wise
18. **b** leader
19. **d** sweltering
20. **a** slowness
21. **c** useless
22. **a** misunderstand
23. **b** support
24. **c** fleeting
25. **d** modern

UNIT 6

1. **a** foul
2. **b** tidy
3. **d** collide
4. **b** distract
5. **c** slight
6. **a** Content
7. **d** policy
8. constant
9. blossomed
10. noble
11. slight
12. quivers
13. drought
14. **c** theme
15. **c** contaminate
16. **b** flutter
17. **d** procedures
18. **a** dryness
19. **d** sidetrack
20. **b** wither
21. **d** lowly
22. **c** small

23. **a** settle
24. **b** compliment
25. **c** faithless

UNIT 7

1. **d** epidemic
2. **c** survive
3. **a** alert
4. **b** penetrate
5. **c** feeble
6. **d** Elementary
7. **a** ancestor
8. alert
9. staples
10. envy
11. romp
12. accurate
13. disaster
14. **b** introductory
15. **b** skip
16. **a** jealousy
17. **d** pierce
18. **d** faint
19. **c** tragedy
20. **c** false
21. **a** perish
22. **b** decendant
23. **d** unnecessary
24. **a** unaware
25. **d** limited

UNIT 8

1. **b** Awkward
2. **d** weary
3. **c** plentiful
4. **a** volunteer
5. **a** reserve
6. **c** scholar
7. **b** smolder
8. gallant
9. ration
10. smoldered
11. lukewarm
12. scholar
13. clatter
14. **d** heroic
15. **a** authority
16. **c** commotion
17. **b** allotment
18. **a** simmer

19. **b** halfhearted
20. **d** energetic
21. **c** meager
22. **a** paid
23. **b** waste
24. **d** graceful
25. **d** race

MASTERY TEST II (UNITS 5–8)

1. lukewarm
2. worthy
3. tidy
4. romp
5. baggage
6. N
7. A
8. V
9. A
10. N
11. V
12. A
13. V
14. N
15. A
16. penetrate
17. alert
18. slight
19. reserve
20. haste
21. weary
22. foul
23. humid
24. envy
25. plentiful

UNIT 9

1. **a** dungeon
2. **b** Gradual
3. **d** discipline
4. **c** uneasy
5. **b** provision
6. **a** nourish
7. **c** Jagged
8. grumble
9. earnest
10. treaty
11. enclose
12. uneasy
13. convict
14. **c** cage
15. **d** correct
16. **b** mutter
17. **a** accord
18. **d** cell

Cycle Two

19. **a** arrangements
20. **c** acquit
21. **b** neglect
22. **d** smooth
23. **b** calm
24. **a** abrupt
25. **c** insincere

UNIT 10

1. **c** proceed
2. **a** unfit
3. **b** sift
4. **d** distress
5. **d** dwell
6. **b** variety
7. **a** spree
8. juvenile
9. outstanding
10. dwell
11. register
12. tardy
13. drenched
14. **a** youthful
15. **c** douse
16. **d** advance
17. **c** binge
18. **c** live
19. **d** separate
20. **b** sameness
21. **a** withdraw
22. **b** proper
23. **c** ordinary
24. **d** early
25. **a** delight

UNIT 11

1. **a** chant
2. **c** reflect
3. **b** heroic
4. **a** site
5. **c** toxic
6. **d** despair
7. **d** lance
8. blockade
9. site
10. extraordinary
11. pointless
12. elevate
13. missionary
14. **d** intone
15. **b** puncture

16. **c** spot
17. **d** bold
18. **b** preacher
19. **a** obstruct
20. **a** hope
21. **d** valuable
22. **c** harmless
23. **a** lower
24. **c** absorb
25. **b** usual

UNIT 12

1. **a** bristle
2. **d** troublesome
3. **c** coarse
4. **b** Marine
5. **a** inspire
6. **c** extreme
7. **d** magnify
8. discard
9. grasp
10. coarse
11. quake
12. focus
13. circular
14. **b** harsh
15. **b** influenced
16. **a** shudder
17. **a** dump
18. **d** seethe
19. **c** excessive
20. **b** straight
21. **d** background
22. **b** land
23. **c** drop
24. **a** reduce
25. **c** easy

MASTERY TEST III
(UNITS 9–12)

1. provision
2. juvenile
3. sift
4. toxic
5. marine
6. V   11. N
7. N   12. N
8. A   13. V
9. V   14. A
10. A   15. N

16. heroic
17. outstanding
18. reflect
19. circular
20. tardy
21. nourish
22. despair
23. discard
24. discipline
25. extraordinary

UNIT 13

1. **b** manufacturer
2. **a** Abstract
3. **b** overthrow
4. **d** ally
5. **c** peculiar
6. **a** Attentive
7. **d** mistrust
8. carefree
9. appoint
10. overthrow
11. courtesy
12. bonus
13. noticeable
14. **c** reward
15. **a** designate
16. **c** politeness
17. **d** lighthearted
18. **b** concoct
19. **b** alert
20. **c** believe
21. **a** support
22. **d** opponent
23. **d** common
24. **b** invisible
25. **c** concrete

UNIT 14

1. **c** compliment
2. **b** Dominant
3. **a** arena
4. **d** Absolute
5. **b** offend
6. **d** dense
7. **b** huddle
8. thorough
9. necessity

Cycle Two

10. hazardous
11. regained
12. huddle
13. absolute
14. **a** solid
15. **c** stadium
16. **a** dangerous
17. **d** main
18. **b** gather
19. **c** careful
20. **d** criticism
21. **a** soothe
22. **c** incomplete
23. **c** lose
24. **a** limited
25. **d** luxury

UNIT 15

1. **d** analyze
2. **c** assist
3. **d** drab
4. **a** merit
5. **a** agile
6. **c** captivity
7. **b** generosity
8. adopt
9. fatal
10. illegal
11. babble
12. genuine
13. assist
14. **b** confinement
15. **d** select
16. **c** jabber
17. **a** evaluate
18. **b** nimble
19. **a** lackluster
20. **d** lawful
21. **b** stinginess
22. **c** shortcomings
23. **d** fake
24. **b** harmless
25. **a** hinder

UNIT 16

1. **a** colossal
2. **d** appropriate
3. **c** symptom
4. **b** hostage
5. **b** assemble

6. **d** scamper
7. **a** effective
8. frail
9. adorn
10. warrant
11. landslide
12. effective
13. rampage
14. **c** prisoner
15. **c** certified
16. **a** frenzy
17. **d** signs
18. **b** decorate
19. **d** avalanche
20. **b** seperate
21. **a** small
22. **c** strong
23. **d** unfitting
24. **c** dawdle
25. **b** useless

MASTERY TEST IV (UNITS 13–16)

1. peculiar
2. dense
3. captivity
4. symptom
5. scamper
6. A   11. V
7. V   12. V
8. N   13. N
9. N   14. V
10. A   15. A
16. adopt
17. landslide
18. absolute
19. offend
20. noticeable
21. effective
22. mistrust
23. necessity
24. analyze
25. illegal

FINAL MASTERY TEST

1. suitable
2. register
3. response
4. magnify

5. appoint
6. establish
7. assist
8. spree
9. collide
10. staple
11. stampede
12. distract
13. dungeon
14. sponsor
15. abstract
16. no change : merit
17. lance
18. no change : ration
19. no change : hostage
20. blockade
21. recall
22. digest
23. jagged
24. deliberate
25. indicate
26. rampage
27. variety
28. sensible
29. **d** heartfelt
30. **b** authority
31. **c** moderate
32. **a** adjust
33. **b** lethal
34. **d** partner
35. **a** occupied
36. **d** strong
37. **b** meaningful
38. **c** deter
39. **d** humble
40. **a** clumsy
41. **b**
42. **a**
43. **d**
44. **c**
45. **c**
46. **a**
47. **b**
48. **d**
49. **c**
50. **a**

VOCABULARY WORKSHOP

LEVEL ORANGE

Jerome Shostak

Sadlier-Oxford
A Division of William H. Sadlier, Inc.
New York, NY 10005-1002

VOCABULARY WORKSHOP

The classic program for:
- developing and enriching vocabulary resources
- promoting more effective communication in today's world
- improving vocabulary skills assessed on standardized tests

Acknowledgments

Corbis Bettman: 19, 43; Macduff Everton: 25; Kevin R. Morris: 31; Peter Johnson: 77; George Hall: 83; David H. Wells: 89.

Stock Market/ Mugshots: 113.

Tony Stone Images/ Alan Thorton: 13; Mark Joseph: 107; Zigy Kaluzny: 119; Cosmo Condina: 125.

Illustrator

Daryl Stevens: 41, 71, 105, 135.

Printed in the United States of America

ISBN: 0-8215-0404-5

3456789/01 00 99

CONTENTS

Foreword 4

The Vocabulary of Vocabulary 5

Pronunciation Key 9

Diagnostic Test 10

Unit One 12

Unit Two 18

Unit Three 24

Unit Four 30

  Review (Units One–Four) 36

Unit Five 42

Unit Six 48

Unit Seven 54

Unit Eight 60

  Review (Units Five–Eight) 66

  Cumulative Review I (Units One–Eight) 72

Unit Nine 76

Unit Ten 82

Unit Eleven 88

Unit Twelve 94

  Review (Units Nine–Twelve) 100

Unit Thirteen 106

Unit Fourteen 112

Unit Fifteen 118

Unit Sixteen 124

  Review (Units Thirteen–Sixteen) 130

  Cumulative Review II (Units Nine–Sixteen) 136

Final Mastery Test 140

Index 144

FOREWORD

For nearly half a century Vocabulary Workshop has proven a highly successful tool for promoting and guiding systematic vocabulary growth. Level Orange, one of two new additions to the Vocabulary Workshop series, is meant both to help younger students *increase* their vocabulary and to *improve* their vocabulary skills. It has also been designed to help prepare students for vocabulary-related items found in standardized tests.

Mastery of the words introduced in this text will make students better readers and better writers—better readers because they will be able to understand and appreciate more of what they read, and better writers because they will have at hand a greater pool of words with which to express themselves. Many of the words introduced in this book are ones that students will encounter in social studies, science, and literature, as well as in their reading outside the classroom.

Word List   Level Orange contains 192 basic words selected on the basis of currency in present-day usage, frequency in recognized vocabulary lists and on standardized tests, and the latest grade-placement research.

Units   The words are grouped in 16 short, stimulating units that include: definitions (with pronunciation and parts of speech), reinforcement of meanings, synonyms and antonyms, in-context sentence completions, and word-association exercises.

Reviews   Four Reviews (one for every four units) reinforce the work of the units with challenging exercises that include Analogies, Vocabulary in Context, and Word Games.

Two Cumulative Reviews, the first covering the first 8 units and the second covering the last 8 units, provide further reinforcement.

Assessment   The Diagnostic Test provides ready assessment of student needs and preparedness at the outset of the term.

The Final Mastery Test provides end-of-term assessment of student achievement.

Teacher Materials   A Teacher's Annotated Edition supplies answers to all of the exercises in the pupil text and an introduction to the Vocabulary Workshop program.

The Supplementary Testing Program provides separate testing exercises covering the material found in the pupil text. Answers are in the Teacher's Annotated Edition.

THE VOCABULARY OF VOCABULARY

English has a large group of special terms to describe how words are used and how they are related to one another. These terms make up what we might call the "vocabulary of vocabulary." Learning to understand and use the "vocabulary of vocabulary" will help you to get better results in your vocabulary-building program.

Part of Speech

Every word in English plays some role in the language. What that role is determines how a word is classified grammatically. These classifications are called "parts of speech." In English there are eight parts of speech: nouns, pronouns, verbs, adjectives, adverbs, prepositions, conjunctions, and interjections. All of the words introduced in this book are nouns (abbreviated *n.*), verbs (*v.*), or adjectives (*adj.*).

A **noun** names a person, place, or thing. *Sister, lake,* and *glass* are nouns. So are *Jefferson, Miami,* and *Olympics.* Nouns also name things such as ideas and feelings; for example, *freedom* and *joy* are nouns.

Verbs express action or a state of being. *Bake, fetch, arrange, lose, hear, think, see, come, sing,* and *know* are verbs.

Adjectives describe or give information about nouns or other adjectives. *Large, red, soft, heavy, old, new, pretty, useful, stormy,* and *glad* are adjectives.

Many English words act as more than one part of speech. The word *light,* for example, can be a verb or a noun. Its part of speech depends upon the way it is used.

NOUN: We saw a *light* in one of the windows. [*light* names a thing]

VERB: I got up to *light* the candles. [*light* expresses an action]

EXERCISES   For each sentence circle the choice that identifies the part of speech of the word in **boldface.**

1. The president gave a **great** speech.
   a. noun   b. verb   (c.) adjective

2. Why don't we **walk** to the store?
   a. noun   (b.) verb   c. adjective

3. It will be a pleasant **walk**.
   (a.) noun   b. verb   c. adjective

4. They slept through the **boring** movie.
   a. noun   b. verb   (c.) adjective

5. He held on with one **hand**.
   (a.) noun   b. verb   c. adjective

6. Please **hand** me the scissors.
   a. noun   (b.) verb   c. adjective

Synonyms and Antonyms

Synonyms

A **synonym** is a word that means *the same* or *nearly the same* as another word.

EXAMPLES

smile — grin	easy — simple
go — leave	scare — frighten
rich — wealthy	heat — warmth

EXERCISES For each of the following groups circle the choice that is most nearly the **same** in meaning as the word in **boldface**.

1. **rescue**	2. **car**	3. **run**	4. **loud**
a. forget	(a.) automobile	a. step	a. dull
(b.) save	b. moped	b. stare	b. sharp
c. pretend	c. aircraft	c. find	(c.) noisy
d. hurry	d. carriage	(d.) dash	d. soft

Antonyms

An **antonym** is a word that is *opposite* or *nearly opposite* in meaning to another word.

EXAMPLES

high — low	win — lose
shout — whisper	pleasure — pain
war — peace	happy — sad

EXERCISES For each of the following groups circle the choice that is most nearly **opposite** in meaning to the word in **boldface**.

1. **forget**	2. **buy**	3. **first**	4. **strength**
a. lose	a. ask	a. big	a. courage
(b.) remember	b. watch	b. small	b. noise
c. tell	(c.) sell	c. best	c. bravery
d. write	d. take	(d.) last	(d.) weakness

Context Clues

When you turn to the "Completing the Sentence" and "Vocabulary in Context" exercises in this book, look for clues built into the passages to guide you to the correct answers. There are three basic types of clues.

Restatement Clues   A restatement clue gives a *definition of*, or a *synonym for*, a missing word.

EXAMPLE   The long walk through the <u>cold</u> rain left me wet and
_____.

    a. thrilled   b. afraid   c. happy   (d.) chilled

Contrast Clues   A contrast clue gives an *antonym for*, or a phrase meaning *the opposite of*, a missing word.

EXAMPLE   Because we did not get to the airport <u>on time</u>, we were
_____ for our flight.

    (a.) late   b. early   c. sleepy   d. ready

Situational Clues   Sometimes the situation itself, as it is outlined in the sentence or passage, suggests the word that is missing but does not state the meaning directly.

EXAMPLE   If you want to wear that <u>torn</u> jacket again, you will have to
_____ it first.

    a. buy   b. wash   (c.) mend   d. iron

To figure out which word is missing from the sentence, ask yourself this question: What would you have to do before you could wear a "torn" jacket again? Would you buy it? wash it? mend it? iron it?

EXERCISES   Use context clues to choose the word that best completes each of the following sentences.

1. To take good _____ of your vegetable garden, you should water it and pull out the weeds.
   (a.) care   b. pictures   c. advantage   d. samples

2. After a week of heavy rain and strong winds, we welcomed the return to _____ and sunny weather.
   a. cloudy   (b.) calm   c. scary   d. foggy

3. To _____ for a test, you should review the lessons in your book and study your class notes.
   a. ask   b. read   c. write   (d.) prepare

Analogies

An **analogy** is a comparison. For example, we can make an analogy, or comparison, between a computer and a human brain.

In this book and in many standardized tests you will be asked to find the relationship between two words. Then, to show that you understand that relationship, you will be asked to choose another pair of words that show the same relationship.

EXAMPLES	1. **light** is to **dark** as	2. **eat** is to **dine** as
	a. sad is to unhappy	a. stand is to sit
	b. windy is to breezy	b. cry is to weep
	c. cold is to hot	c. mend is to tear
	d. wet is to damp	d. run is to walk

In the first example, note that *light* and *dark* are **antonyms**; they are opposite in meaning. Of the four choices given, which pair is made up of words that are also antonyms, or opposite in meaning? The answer, of course, is *c, cold is to hot.*

In the second example, note that *eat* and *dine* are **synonyms**; they have nearly the same meaning. Of the four choices given, which pair is made up of words that are also synonyms, or have nearly the same meaning? The answer is *b, cry is to weep.*

There are many other kinds of analogies besides ones based on synonyms and antonyms. For each of the exercises that follow, first study carefully the pair of words in **boldface**. Then, when you have figured out the relationship between the two words, look for another pair that has the same relationship. Circle the item that best completes the analogy, and then write the relationship on the lines provided.

3. **tulip** is to **flower** as

a. apple is to fruit *(circled)*

b. chalk is to crayon

c. wood is to table

d. bird is to crow

Relationship: **A tulip is a type of flower; an apple is a type of fruit.**

4. **bat** is to **baseball** as

a. field is to soccer

b. coach is to team

c. ticket is to game

d. stick is to hockey *(circled)*

Relationship: **A bat is used in baseball; a stick is used in hockey.**

5. **hat** is to **head** as

a. scarf is to gloves

b. wool is to sweater

c. shoe is to foot *(circled)*

d. sleeve is to shirt

Relationship: **A hat is worn on the head; a shoe is worn on the foot.**

PRONUNCIATION KEY

The pronunciation is given for every basic word introduced in this book. The symbols, which are shown below, are similar to those that appear in most standard dictionaries. The author has consulted a large number of dictionaries for this purpose but has relied primarily on *Webster's Third New International Dictionary* and *The Random House Dictionary of the English Language (Unabridged)*.

Of course there are many English words, including some that appear in this book, for which two (or more) pronunciations are commonly accepted. In virtually all cases where such words occur in this book, students are given just one pronunciation. Exceptions to this rule are made, however, in cases when the pronunciation of a word changes according to its part of speech. For example, as a noun the word *object* is pronounced 'äb jekt; as a verb it is pronounced əb 'jekt. It is believed that these relatively simple pronunciation guides will be readily usable by students. It should be emphasized, however, that the best way to learn the pronunciation of a word is to listen to and imitate an educated speaker.

Vowels	ā	lake	e	stress	ü	boot, new
	a	mat	ī	knife	ù	foot, pull
	â	care	i	sit	ə	rug, broken
	ä	bark, bottle	ō	flow	ər	bird, better
	aù	doubt	ô	all, cord		
	ē	beat, wordy	oi	oil		

Consonants	ch	child, lecture	s	cellar	wh	what
	g	give	sh	shun	y	yell
	j	gentle, bridge	th	thank	z	is
	ŋ	sing	t̶h̶	those	zh	measure

All other consonants are sounded as in the alphabet.

Stress	The accent mark *precedes* the syllable receiving the major stress: en 'rich

Diagnostic Test

For each of the following items circle the letter for the word or phrase that best expresses the meaning of the word in **boldface** in the introductory phrase.

Example
asked for a **hint**
a. job   (b.) clue   c. napkin   d. book

1. **thaw** the frozen fields
   a. plow   (b.) warm   c. cross   d. graze

2. follow our **policy**
   (a.) guidelines   b. clues   c. instincts   d. leaders

3. **oppose** the decision
   a. agree with   b. wait for   c. listen to   (d.) fight against

4. write an **outstanding** composition
   a. long   b. short   c. good   (d.) excellent

5. **scamper** on the grass
   (a.) run around   b. sit still   c. lie down   d. drink tea

6. a **coarse** washcloth
   a. clean   b. old   c. worn   (d.) rough

7. pick up my **baggage**
   a. wrappers   b. lunch trays   (c.) suitcases   d. clothes

8. **trudge** to school
   a. skip happily   b. ride swiftly   (c.) walk slowly   d. drive carefully

9. a **noticeable** dent in the car
   a. tiny   (b.) visible   c. new   d. old

10. **drench** our clothes
    a. find   b. deliver   c. stain   (d.) soak

11. **merit** a reward
    a. return   b. receive   (c.) earn   d. present

12. the **babble** of the brook

   a. length   (b.) gurgle   c. color   d. current

13. **survive** the shipwreck

   a. hear about   b. hope for   c. swim by   (d.) live through

14. began to feel **drowsy**

   (a.) sleepy   b. sad   c. angry   d. happy

15. **adorn** with sparkling jewels

   a. spoil   (b.) decorate   c. ruin   d. leave

16. seemed to be **uneasy**

   a. tired   b. relaxed   c. thoughtful   (d.) embarrassed

17. **offend** the whole audience

   a. please   (b.) anger   c. fear   d. delight

18. the **essential** ingredient

   a. expensive   b. delicious   c. rare   (d.) main

19. **grasp** the bike's handlebars

   a. paint   b. remove   c. break   (d.) grab

20. known for their **noble** deeds

   a. many   b. wicked   (c.) remarkable   d. selfish

21. **elevate** your broken foot

   (a.) raise   b. bandage   c. heal   d. forget

22. **stun** the onlookers

   a. amuse   (b.) shock   c. praise   d. watch

23. gave an honest **response**

   (a.) answer   b. try   c. excuse   d. story

24. the **annual** school picnic

   a. indoor   b. important   (c.) yearly   d. outdoor

25. heard the **clatter** in the kitchen

   (a.) clanking   b. dripping   c. laughter   d. speech

UNIT 1

Definitions

Study the spelling, pronunciation, part of speech, and definition given for each of the words below. Write the word in the blank space in the sentence that follows. Then read the synonyms and antonyms.

1. **celebrity**
   (sə 'le brə tē)

   (n.) a well-known person; someone who is famous; fame
   Her popular paintings have made her a _____ celebrity _____ in the art world.

   SYNONYMS: a star; fame
   ANTONYMS: an unknown, nobody; anonymity

2. **counsel**
   ('kaùn səl)

   (n.) opinions or ideas given for a plan of action; a talk that leads to a decision; a lawyer
   The head of the law firm is serving as the lead _____ counsel _____ for this trial.

   (v.) to give advice or an opinion; to offer help
   After we lost a very close game, our coach tried to _____ counsel _____ us on how to accept defeat.

   SYNONYMS: advice, wisdom, guidance; a lawyer; to help, advise, recommend

3. **demonstrate**
   ('dem ən strāt)

   (v.) to clearly explain, show or prove with examples, models, or experiments; to gather in public to support an opinion or cause
   To become a band member you must _____ demonstrate _____ some musical skill.

   SYNONYMS: to show, model, prove, illustrate, reveal
   ANTONYM: to hide

4. **drowsy**
   ('draù zē)

   (adj.) ready to fall asleep, sleepy
   After eating that big dinner, I felt too _____ drowsy _____ to read.

   SYNONYMS: sleepy, tired, sluggish
   ANTONYMS: alert, wakeful

5. **essential**
   (i 'sen chəl)

   (adj.) of the highest importance, necessary
   Food, water, and shelter are _____ essential _____ to survival.

   (n.) something necessary or very important
   When you pack for a long trip, start with the _____ essentials _____.

   SYNONYMS: necessary, vital, key, basic
   ANTONYMS: unimportant, minor, unnecessary

6. **hardship**
   ('härd ship)

   (n.) something that causes suffering or difficulty; a condition that is hard to bear
   The pioneers had to live with many a _____ hardship _____.

   SYNONYMS: a burden, ordeal, misfortune
   ANTONYM: ease, comfort

12

Tractor-trailer rigs **haul** (word 7) goods over the nation's interstate highway system.

7. haul
(hôl)

(v.) to move by pulling, dragging, or carting, sometimes in a vehicle; to apply force to transport something

A truck came to _____ haul _____ away the trash.

(n.) the amount taken or won at one time

The boat brought in a good _____ haul _____ of fish.

SYNONYMS: to lug, pull, cart, drag, carry, lift, tug; a yield, catch

8. humble
('həm bəl)

(adj.) low in rank or position; plain, not proud or grand

The family lived in a _____ humble _____ cottage.

(v.) to take away one's spirit, power, fame, or independence

What will it take to _____ humble _____ the proud king?

SYNONYMS: modest, simple, plain, earthy; to shame, embarrass
ANTONYMS: bold, grand; to empower, raise up

9. pledge
(plej)

(n.) something given as a sign of a promise, especially money meant for a good cause; a sign or promise to fulfill an agreement

We can give a _____ pledge _____ of ten dollars to the fund.

(v.) to promise

A bride and groom _____ pledge _____ to honor each other.

SYNONYMS: a promise, guarantee; to vow, swear, vouch

10. sincere
(sin 'sēr)

(adj.) without pretending; with honesty and real feeling

They offered a _____ sincere _____ apology.

SYNONYMS: genuine, true, heartfelt
ANTONYMS: false, phony

11. stampede
(stam 'pēd)

(n.) a wild rush of animals or people, usually when frightened

The flood forced a _____ stampede _____ of cattle to higher ground.

(v.) to run away or cause to scatter in a wild manner, often in panic; to rush forward together as a crowd

The fans began to _____ stampede _____ toward the stage.

SYNONYMS: a flight, rush, dash; to bolt, charge, panic
ANTONYMS: to stroll, wander

12. suitable
('sü tə bəl)

(adj.) just right or appropriate; well matched

I'm going shopping for a _____ suitable _____ outfit to wear.

SYNONYMS: appropriate, proper, fitting, right
ANTONYMS: inappropriate, mismatched, improper

Match the Meaning

For each item below choose the word whose meaning is suggested by the clue given. Then write the word in the space provided.

1. A forest fire made the frightened herd _____**stampede**_____ toward the river.
   a. demonstrate   b. stampede   c. pledge   d. haul

2. To offer helpful advice is to give _____**counsel**_____.
   a. counsel   b. haul   c. celebrity   d. pledge

3. Something that brings suffering is called a _____**hardship**_____.
   a. hardship   b. celebrity   c. counsel   d. pledge

4. By 10 P.M., we were too tired and _____**drowsy**_____ to play chess.
   a. humble   b. sincere   c. drowsy   d. suitable

5. Bread is _____**essential**_____ for making sandwiches.
   a. humble   b. sincere   c. drowsy   d. essential

6. Watch carefully as I _____**demonstrate**_____ how to make tacos.
   a. counsel   b. demonstrate   c. pledge   d. stampede

7. To give a promise is to make a _____**pledge**_____.
   a. stampede   b. haul   c. pledge   d. hardship

8. Losing may _____**humble**_____ that boastful coach.
   a. demonstrate   b. haul   c. counsel   d. humble

9. One way to move a heavy box is to _____**haul**_____ it on a wagon.
   a. demonstrate   b. stampede   c. haul   d. pledge

10. People who mean what they say are _____**sincere**_____.
    a. sincere   b. essential   c. drowsy   d. suitable

11. Famous people don't always enjoy their _____**celebrity**_____.
    a. pledge   b. stampede   c. hardship   d. celebrity

12. A(n) _____**suitable**_____ gift is one that fits the occasion perfectly.
    a. humble   b. essential   c. suitable   d. drowsy

Synonyms

For each item below choose the word that is most nearly the **same** in meaning as the word or phrase in **boldface**. Then write your choice on the line provided.

1. thanked her for her **guidance**
   a. celebrity   b. pledge   c. counsel   d. stampede   _____counsel_____

2. **promise** to repay the loan
   a. pledge   b. counsel   c. demonstrate d. haul   _____pledge_____

3. **drag** the stuffed suitcase
   a. haul   b. counsel   c. pledge   d. stampede   _____haul_____

4. **modest** words of a simple prayer
   a. essential   b. suitable   c. drowsy   d. humble   _____humble_____

5. **showed** how to dive
   a. demonstrated b. stampeded   c. pledged   d. hauled   _____demonstrated_____

6. bring **appropriate** clothing
   a. humble   b. sincere   c. drowsy   d. suitable   _____suitable_____

Antonyms

For each item below choose the word that is most nearly **opposite** in meaning to the word or phrase in **boldface**. Then write your choice on the line provided.

1. a life of **ease**
   a. counsel   b. pledge   c. stampede   d. hardship   _____hardship_____

2. a **false** smile
   a. essential   b. drowsy   c. sincere   d. humble   _____sincere_____

3. found an **unimportant** clue
   a. sincere   b. essential   c. humble   d. suitable   _____essential_____

4. **unknowns** in the crowd
   a. stampedes   b. counsels   c. hardships   d. celebrities   _____celebrities_____

5. was **alert** during the movie
   a. sincere   b. humble   c. drowsy   d. suitable   _____drowsy_____

6. **stroll** down the ramp
   a. demonstrate b. stampede   c. pledge   d. counsel   _____stampede_____

Completing the Sentence

From the list of words on pages 12–13, choose the one that best completes each item below. Then write the word in the space provided. (You may have to change the word's ending.)

THE VISITING FOLKSINGER

■ We are excited that a real _____ **celebrity** _____ is coming to visit our class. It's not very often that we have the chance to meet someone so famous.

■ "We want to welcome our guest warmly, but let's not _____ **stampede** _____ to the door. Someone might get hurt!" our teacher said.

■ Our visitor sings songs about his _____ **humble** _____ hometown—the same modest little town where our teacher grew up.

■ The _____ **hardships** _____ they experienced then are hard for us to imagine today. Compared to the difficulties they faced, we have it pretty easy.

RIGHTS IN AMERICA

■ In America, one of our _____ **essential** _____ freedoms is the right to free speech. Some people consider it our most important right.

■ Our laws allow people to _____ **demonstrate** _____ in public, even to support an unpopular cause.

■ People can get legal _____ **counsel** _____ if they believe their rights have been taken away.

■ It's up to the courts to decide if the complaints are _____ **sincere** _____ or phony. If a judge believes that a complaint is made up, he or she may throw it out.

MEDICAL RESEARCH

■ The scientists made a _____ **pledge** _____ to publish the results of their experiments fully and honestly.

■ They will study whether a new medicine is _____ **suitable** _____ for children. If it is found to be appropriate, the medicine should be in drug stores next year.

■ It's amazing how much equipment they _____ **haul** _____ into the lab! It must have taken a big truck to deliver it all.

■ The scientists often work late, but they stop when they get too _____ **drowsy** _____ to concentrate.

Word Associations

*Circle the letter next to the word or expression that best completes the sentence or answers the question. Pay special attention to the word in **boldface**.*

1. Which of the following is probably a **celebrity**?
   a. a star baseball player
   b. a nurse
   c. a local plumber
   d. a florist

2. If you need **counsel**, you might
   a. take a nap
   b. walk the dog
   c. call a lawyer
   d. wash the dishes

3. We might see a **drowsy** person
   a. stretched out on the couch
   b. going jogging
   c. starting a difficult project
   d. hanging wallpaper

4. A **pledge** should be
   a. honest
   b. difficult
   c. funny
   d. false

5. To **haul** a pony, you would use a
   a. skateboard
   b. horse trailer
   c. backpack
   d. fire engine

6. A **suitable** item for the pool is
   a. a snowshoe
   b. a piano
   c. a towel
   d. toothpaste

7. A real **hardship** for a goldfish would be to have
   a. a boring fishbowl
   b. a purple fishbowl
   c. an empty fishbowl
   d. a square fishbowl

8. A **humble** person might say
   a. "I deserve more!"
   b. "I don't deserve it."
   c. "Show me the prize!"
   d. "I'm number one!"

9. An **essential** part of a parade is
   a. cotton candy
   b. a rainy day
   c. a marching band
   d. a bunch of roses

10. I can best **demonstrate** ballet
   a. in a phone booth
   b. on a stage
   c. in a shoe store
   d. on the radio

11. A **sincere** person would
   a. play a trick on you
   b. get you a present
   c. tell you the truth
   d. throw a party

12. Why might crowds **stampede**?
   a. They are tired.
   b. They are bored.
   c. They are curious.
   d. They are afraid.

Definitions

Study the spelling, pronunciation, part of speech, and definition given for each of the words below. Write the word in the blank space in the sentence that follows. Then read the synonyms and antonyms.

1. **annual**
   ('an yü əl)

   (adj.) coming each year; once a year; lasting a year
   The _____ annual _____ class picnic is planned for the last week of the school year.

   (n.) a book or magazine that comes out once a year; a plant that lives or lasts for just one growing season
   One of my poems will appear in the 1998 poetry _____ annual _____.

   SYNONYMS: yearly; a yearbook

2. **basic**
   ('bā sik)

   (adj.) having to do with the main or starting point of something
   We understand the _____ basic _____ idea of the game.

   (n., usually plural) a key element or part
   I got the _____ basics _____ of addition in first grade.

   SYNONYMS: essential, key, primary, fundamental

3. **competition**
   (käm pə 'ti shən)

   (n.) trying to outdo others; a game or contest
   I am planning to enter the kite-flying _____ competition _____.

   SYNONYMS: a contest, rivalry, match, test
   ANTONYM: cooperation

4. **contract**
   (n., 'kän trakt;
   v., kən 'trakt)

   (n.) an agreement or understanding that can be enforced by law; a document that explains legal conditions
   Many people who buy computers also buy a service _____ contract _____.

   (v.) to make or grow smaller; to come down with, as a sickness
   Some soft woods _____ contract _____ when they dry.

   SYNONYMS: an agreement, arrangement, deal, pact; to shrink; to catch, get
   ANTONYMS: to expand, enlarge

5. **dismiss**
   (dis 'mis)

   (v.) to send away or permit to leave; to remove from a job; to stop thinking about
   Our teacher will not _____ dismiss _____ the class until we are all quiet.

   SYNONYMS: to reject, fire, drop, discharge
   ANTONYMS: to hire, hold, consider, employ

6. **neglect**
   (ni 'glekt)

   (v.) to hold back care or attention; to fail to follow through
   You won't do well in school if you _____ neglect _____ your homework.

   (n.) a steady lack of care, often because of carelessness or laziness
   Our rose garden suffers from _____ neglect _____.

   SYNONYMS: to ignore, disregard, overlook, forget; inattention
   ANTONYM: to pamper

Because they had to remain very still for long exposures, the subjects of early photographs often appear **stern** (word 11). Shown here is John Quincy Adams, the first President to be photographed.

7. obtain
(əb 'tān)

(v.) to get or gain through some effort
Customers can _____obtain_____ *rare coins in that shop.*

SYNONYMS: to acquire, gather
ANTONYMS: to lose, forgo

8. portion
('pōr shən)

(n.) a section or piece; a part of the whole; a serving of food
I'll have a small _____portion_____ *of soup.*

SYNONYMS: a part, share, helping
ANTONYM: a whole

9. recall
(v., ri 'kôl;
n., 'rē kôl)

(v.) to bring back to mind; to remind one; to ask to return
Photographs help us _____recall_____ *highlights of our trip.*

(n.) the ability or act of remembering
He had no _____recall_____ *at all of the story.*

SYNONYMS: to remember, resemble; to revoke; a memory, recollection
ANTONYM: to forget

10. sponsor
('spän sər)

(n.) one who helps or takes responsibility for another person or group; a person or business that pays for an ad on radio or television
A generous _____sponsor_____ *paid for new uniforms for everyone in the band.*

(v.) to act as a sponsor to a group, person, or event
Many businesses _____sponsor_____ *the Special Olympics.*

SYNONYMS: a supporter, backer, provider; to support

11. stern
(stərn)

(adj.) not kindly or gentle; harsh-looking
The officer gave them a _____stern_____ *warning.*

(n.) the back end of a boat
You can climb the ladder in the _____stern_____ *.*

SYNONYMS: harsh, sharp, severe, firm, strict, grim; the rear
ANTONYMS: gentle, tender, kindly; the bow

12. vacant
('vā kənt)

(adj.) not used, filled, or lived in; without thought or expression
This bus has no more _____vacant_____ *seats.*

SYNONYMS: empty, unused, available, open; blank
ANTONYMS: full; occupied

19

Match the Meaning

For each item below choose the word whose meaning is suggested by the clue given. Then write the word in the space provided.

1. A weak memory leaves me with little or no ___**recall**___.
   a. neglect   b. competition   c. recall   d. sponsor

2. The main point of a story is its ___**basic**___ idea.
   a. annual   b. basic   c. stern   d. vacant

3. If you study hard, you will ___**obtain**___ a good grade.
   a. sponsor   b. obtain   c. dismiss   d. neglect

4. A ___**contract**___ is a legal paper that people sign.
   a. sponsor   b. recall   c. competition   d. contract

5. Camping sites with no tents on them are ___**vacant**___.
   a. stern   b. vacant   c. annual   d. basic

6. If you ___**neglect**___ to water the flowers, they'll droop and die.
   a. neglect   b. dismiss   c. contract   d. recall

7. The Olympics is a ___**competition**___ that attracts the world's best athletes.
   a. sponsor   b. contract   c. competition   d. portion

8. We can also call a part a ___**portion**___.
   a. portion   b. contract   c. recall   d. competition

9. A once-a-year trip is a(n) ___**annual**___ event.
   a. annual   b. basic   c. vacant   d. stern

10. To pay for a television show is to ___**sponsor**___ it.
    a. sponsor   b. contract   c. recall   d. neglect

11. A person who is harsh and strict might be called ___**stern**___.
    a. annual   b. vacant   c. basic   d. stern

12. If I ___**dismiss**___ an idea, I stop thinking about it.
    a. obtain   b. contract   c. dismiss   d. recall

Synonyms

For each item below choose the word that is most nearly the **same** in meaning as the word or phrase in **boldface**. Then write your choice on the line provided.

1. **acquire** a set of paints
   a. recall   b. obtain   c. neglect   d. dismiss   _____obtain_____

2. the **key** facts of their argument
   a. vacant   b. basic   c. stern   d. annual   _____basic_____

3. **fire** that careless truck driver
   a. dismiss   b. recall   c. neglect   d. portion   _____dismiss_____

4. my **share** of the reward
   a. portion   b. contract   c. recall   d. competition   _____portion_____

5. the high school **yearbook**
   a. contract   b. sponsor   c. annual   d. competition   _____annual_____

6. a **supporter** of the local dance company
   a. contract   b. sponsor   c. portion   d. neglect   _____sponsor_____

Antonyms

For each item below choose the word that is most nearly **opposite** in meaning to the word or phrase in **boldface**. Then write your choice on the line provided.

1. a **kindly** gaze
   a. vacant   b. basic   c. stern   d. annual   _____stern_____

2. **expand** its wings
   a. obtain   b. dismiss   c. recall   d. contract   _____contract_____

3. an **occupied** seat
   a. vacant   b. annual   c. basic   d. stern   _____vacant_____

4. **forget** the words to the song
   a. dismiss   b. recall   c. obtain   d. neglect   _____recall_____

5. **cooperation** among players
   a. contract   b. competition   c. portion   d. neglect   _____competition_____

6. **pamper** my best friend
   a. sponsor   b. dismiss   c. neglect   d. recall   _____neglect_____

Completing the Sentence

From the list of words on pages 18–19, choose the one that best completes each item below. Then write the word in the space provided. (You may have to change the word's ending.)

THAT'S S-P-E-L-L-I-N-G . . .

■ The National Spelling Bee is a(n) _____**annual**_____ event that takes place each spring in Washington, D.C.

■ The Spelling Bee's _____**sponsor**_____ is a company that owns newspapers and television stations.

■ This nationwide _____**competition**_____ is open to students through eighth grade. Thousands of students enter the spelling contest. They study long and hard to prepare for the event.

■ Interested students can _____**obtain**_____ an official booklet that gives the words they may be asked to spell.

A GREEN PROJECT

■ Neighbors came up with a good way to use a(n) _____**vacant**_____ city lot on their block. The lot had been empty since a fire had destroyed the building that had stood there.

■ "Let's try to turn at least a(n) _____**portion**_____ of it into a community garden," they said, "even if it is only a small part."

■ They wrote up a(n) _____**contract**_____ between themselves and the city to let them use some of the space as long as they would do all the work.

■ At first, city officials wanted to _____**dismiss**_____ the idea. They rejected the plan because they thought it might cost too much money.

■ But when local businesses agreed to donate _____**basic**_____ equipment, such as shovels, rakes, and seeds, the plan was approved.

POLLUTION SOLUTION

■ Air quality in some parts of the country got so bad that the government issued _____**stern**_____ warnings and began to pass strong anti-pollution laws.

■ The government threatened to force manufacturers to _____**recall**_____ cars and other machines that added too much pollution to the air. Most companies tried to make their products run more cleanly.

■ But companies that chose to _____**neglect**_____ the warnings had to pay large fines for ignoring the new laws.

22 ■ Unit 2

Word Associations

*Circle the letter next to the word or expression that best completes the sentence or answers the question. Pay special attention to the word in **boldface**.*

1. Which is *not* an **annual** event?
   a. your birthday
   b. the Fourth of July
   c. Thanksgiving
   d. the Winter Olympics ⟵

2. Before a big **competition**, you
   a. should practice or study ⟵
   b. should arrive an hour late
   c. should start a scrapbook
   d. should take a vacation

3. You might **dismiss** a pet-sitter
   a. who sang silly songs
   b. who fed the pets
   c. who ignored the pets ⟵
   d. who made a telephone call

4. Which is *not* a **basic** need?
   a. food
   b. music ⟵
   c. shelter
   d. clothing

5. Which might you **contract**?
   a. a dog house
   b. the chicken pox ⟵
   c. a pony ride
   d. a wild goose chase

6. One way to **obtain** a fossil is to
   a. buy one at a museum shop ⟵
   b. draw one in your notebook
   c. read about one in a book
   d. write a letter to the mayor

7. Workers who **neglect** their jobs
   a. might get fired ⟵
   b. might earn raises
   c. might win promotions
   d. might receive gifts

8. A fair **portion** of a shared lunch
   a. is a bite of a cookie
   b. is half of a sandwich ⟵
   c. is all the chocolate pudding
   d. is a spoonful of yogurt

9. We **recall** the party when we see
   a. a bowl of oatmeal
   b. a math test
   c. a bunch of balloons ⟵
   d. a rocket launch

10. A **sponsor** might be willing to
    a. give you a job ⟵
    b. learn your favorite dance
    c. borrow money from you
    d. listen to your radio

11. Where is the **stern** of a ship?
    a. at the front
    b. at the back ⟵
    c. at the side
    d. at the center

12. A **vacant** apartment has
    a. no air conditioning
    b. nobody living in it ⟵
    c. roomy closets
    d. very expensive rent

Definitions

Study the spelling, pronunciation, part of speech, and definition given for each of the words below. Write the word in the blank space in the sentence that follows. Then read the synonyms and antonyms.

1. **attractive**
   (ə 'trak tiv)

   (adj.) pleasing to the eye, mind, or senses; having the power to draw attention

   Most people notice someone with an _____**attractive**_____ *smile.*

   SYNONYMS: appealing, likable, charming, beautiful, inviting
   ANTONYMS: unappealing, unpleasant, disagreeable, offensive

2. **burden**
   ('bər dən)

   (n.) something that is carried, a load; something that is very hard to bear

   It is a _____**burden**_____ *to keep a secret.*

   (v.) to weigh down or put too heavy a load on

   I am sorry to _____**burden**_____ *you with all of these heavy packages.*

   SYNONYMS: a weight, baggage, difficulty, hardship, worry; to load, afflict, oppress
   ANTONYMS: a relief; to relieve, lighten

3. **consent**
   (kən 'sent)

   (v.) to agree to or approve; to give permission

   My parents would not _____**consent**_____ *to my staying up late.*

   (n.) approval or permission

   The teacher needs our parents' _____**consent**_____ *so that we can go on the class trip.*

   SYNONYMS: to allow, permit, accept; agreement, authorization
   ANTONYMS: to disapprove, refuse, deny, disallow; refusal, denial

4. **dependable**
   (di 'pen də bəl)

   (adj.) capable of being relied on; trustworthy

   A taxi driver needs a _____**dependable**_____ *car that always starts, even in bad weather.*

   SYNONYMS: trustworthy, reliable, responsible
   ANTONYMS: unreliable, undependable, untrustworthy

5. **indicate**
   ('in də kāt)

   (v.) to point to or point out; to be a sign of; to state or express briefly

   The nurse told me that a skin rash may _____**indicate**_____ *an allergy or an insect bite.*

   SYNONYMS: to mark, show, signify, suggest, announce
   ANTONYM: to conceal

6. **previous**
   ('prē vē əs)

   (adj.) coming before in time or order

   Our teacher asked us to please turn back to the _____**previous**_____ *page.*

   SYNONYMS: earlier, preceding, prior, past
   ANTONYMS: following, later, succeeding

Because they are often used to carry heavy loads, mules are sometimes called "beasts of **burden**" (word 2).

7. **qualify**
('kwä lə fī)

(v.) to be or become fit for something; to limit or narrow the meaning of
You must be eighteen years old to _____qualify_____ *to vote in a national election.*

SYNONYMS: to authorize, entitle, prepare, suit; to limit, modify

8. **response**
(ri 'späns)

(n.) a reply or answer; a reaction to something
I am still waiting for a _____response_____ *to my letter.*

SYNONYMS: an answer, acknowledgement, reaction

9. **shabby**
('sha bē)

(adj.) worn or faded from use or wear; dressed in worn-out clothes; not fair or generous
The child shivered in the _____shabby_____ *old coat.*

SYNONYMS: ragged, run-down; mean, wretched; unkind
ANTONYMS: elegant, grand; lavish; generous, kind

10. **thaw**
(thô)

(v.) to melt or cause to melt; to warm up gradually
Let the turkey _____thaw_____ *in the refrigerator before you cook it.*
(n.) a period of weather warm enough to melt ice and snow
We had an early _____thaw_____ *in January.*

SYNONYMS: to melt, liquefy
ANTONYMS: to freeze, solidify

11. **urgent**
('ər jənt)

(adj.) needing or demanding immediate action or attention
The fire department answered an _____urgent_____ *call for help.*

SYNONYMS: critical, pressing, immediate
ANTONYMS: unimportant, minor

12. **vanity**
('va nə tē)

(n.) the quality of being stuck-up or vain; having too much pride in one's looks or abilities; a dressing table
A person's display of _____vanity_____ *can be very annoying.*

SYNONYMS: conceit, arrogance, pride
ANTONYMS: modesty, humility

Match the Meaning

For each item below, choose the word whose meaning is suggested by the clue given. Then write the word in the space provided.

1. The day before this one was the _____**previous**_____ day.
   a. previous   b. urgent   c. dependable   d. shabby

2. A heavy responsibility can be a _____**burden**_____.
   a. consent   b. burden   c. response   d. vanity

3. Our class got the principal's _____**consent**_____ to start a recycling project.
   a. thaw   b. burden   c. consent   d. vanity

4. Ice will _____**thaw**_____ when the temperature gets above the freezing point.
   a. thaw   b. consent   c. qualify   d. indicate

5. Signs on highways _____**indicate**_____ where the exits are.
   a. thaw   b. qualify   c. indicate   d. consent

6. You can always count on _____**dependable**_____ people.
   a. urgent   b. shabby   c. attractive   d. dependable

7. You must be sixteen to _____**qualify**_____ for a driver's license.
   a. thaw   b. burden   c. indicate   d. qualify

8. Too much pride in your own looks or abilities is _____**vanity**_____.
   a. response   b. vanity   c. burden   d. consent

9. A faded and torn chair could be described as _____**shabby**_____.
   a. previous   b. dependable   c. shabby   d. attractive

10. _____**Attractive**_____ window displays will draw the attention of shoppers.
    a. Attractive   b. Shabby   c. Urgent   d. Dependable

11. An _____**urgent**_____ problem calls for quick action.
    a. attractive   b. previous   c. shabby   d. urgent

12. When someone asks you a question, you should give a _____**response**_____.
    a. response   b. vanity   c. burden   d. thaw

Synonyms

For each item below choose the word that is most nearly the **same** in meaning as the word or phrase in **boldface.** Then write your choice on the line provided.

1. the beggar's **ragged** clothing
   a. previous   b. dependable   c. shabby   d. attractive   _____shabby_____

2. the **pressure** of many responsibilities
   a. vanity   b. burden   c. response   d. thaw   _____burden_____

3. an **appealing** display of flowers
   a. dependable   b. shabby   c. attractive   d. urgent   _____attractive_____

4. **certified** to fly an airplane
   a. thawed   b. burdened   c. qualified   d. indicated   _____qualified_____

5. received an **answer** to my letter
   a. response   b. burden   c. vanity   d. consent   _____response_____

6. our **agreement** to host the party
   a. response   b. thaw   c. vanity   d. consent   _____consent_____

Antonyms

For each item below choose the word that is most nearly **opposite** in meaning to the word or phrase in **boldface.** Then write your choice on the line provided.

1. an **unimportant** message
   a. previous   b. dependable   c. urgent   d. attractive   _____urgent_____

2. **unreliable** information
   a. previous   b. urgent   c. shabby   d. dependable   _____dependable_____

3. the **following** question
   a. urgent   b. attractive   c. previous   d. shabby   _____previous_____

4. began to **freeze**
   a. indicate   b. qualify   c. consent   d. thaw   _____thaw_____

5. **concealed** the path to the lake
   a. indicated   b. qualified   c. thawed   d. burdened   _____indicated_____

6. a show of **modesty**
   a. vanity   b. response   c. burden   d. consent   _____vanity_____

Completing the Sentence

From the list of words on pages 24–25, choose the one that best completes each item below. Write the word in the space provided. (You may have to change the word's ending.)

From the list of words on pages 24–25,

UNEXPECTED DANGER

■ When the hikers set out for the mountain, the weather was just as fine as it had been the _____ **previous** _____ day. Little did they know the danger that lay in store for them.

■ They did not realize how _____ **shabby** _____ their clothes and boots were until an unexpected blizzard hit. The temperature dropped sharply, and their worn-out clothes did not keep them warm.

■ Shivering and lost, they knew how _____ **urgent** _____ it was to find shelter from the storm.

■ At last they came to a cabin. They knocked on the door but got no _____ **response** _____ .

■ Then they tried the door, and it opened. Once they were inside, the hikers began to _____ **thaw** _____ themselves by the wood stove.

■ They used towels they found stored in a _____ **vanity** _____ to dry themselves off. Before the hikers left the cabin, they wrote a note thanking the cabin's owner.

ADOPTING A PET

■ For months we asked our parents to agree to let us get a dog. We were very excited when they finally _____ **consented** _____ to let us have one.

■ "We'll be very _____ **dependable** _____ pet owners," we promised. "We'll feed the dog and walk it and play with it every day."

■ "If I notice anything to _____ **indicate** _____ that you are not taking good care of the dog, we will have to give it away," our dad warned.

■ At the pound the vet asked us lots of questions to find out whether we were fit to adopt a dog. We found that not all people _____ **qualify** _____ .

■ "Some pets can be a _____ **burden** _____ ," she explained. "Good intentions are not enough. But you seem ready to accept the responsibility."

■ We looked at a lot of dogs before we found the one that was right for us. We think we picked the most _____ **attractive** _____ dog there, one with beautiful golden fur and sparkling brown eyes.

Word Associations

*Circle the letter next to the word or expression that best completes the sentence or answers the question. Pay special attention to the word in **boldface**.*

1. To **indicate** a place on a map, you might
   a. take a picture of it
   b. look it up in an atlas
   (c.) point it out
   d. write down its name

2. Which is *not* **attractive** to cats?
   a. some fish
   b. some birds
   c. some catnip
   (d.) some dogs

3. Don't expect **consent** for a class
   a. poetry reading
   b. meeting
   (c.) fireworks display
   d. project

4. A **dependable** TV would
   (a.) work all the time
   b. have wavy or rolling lines
   c. break down
   d. blow a fuse

5. If it is May, the **previous** month
   a. was June
   b. was March
   (c.) was April
   d. was July

6. To **qualify** for a gold medal, you must
   a. have neat handwriting
   (b.) win the race
   c. speak Latin
   d. have no brothers or sisters

7. A sensible **response** to the question "How are you?" is
   a. "Ten o'clock."
   b. "Some pizza, please."
   (c.) "Just fine, thanks."
   d. "No thank you."

8. **Shabby** behavior might include
   a. making a new friend
   b. sharing your toys
   (c.) making rude comments
   d. giving away old clothes

9. Which is an **urgent** situation?
   a. no more popcorn
   (b.) a grease fire in the kitchen
   c. a chipped fingernail
   d. a sad song on the radio

10. During a March **thaw**, you might
    (a.) hope spring will arrive early
    b. shovel snow
    c. go swimming in a lake
    d. go ice-skating on a pond

11. You may accuse me of **vanity** if I
    a. help you do your homework
    b. let you borrow my math book
    c. draw a good picture of a horse
    (d.) boast about my many talents

12. Which is a **burden** to carry?
    a. a ruler
    (b.) a heavy suitcase
    c. a lunch box
    d. a pair of shoes

UNIT 4

Definitions

Study the spelling, pronunciation, part of speech, and definition given for each of the words below. Write the word in the blank space in the sentence that follows. Then read the synonyms and antonyms.

1. **ambush**
   ('am bùsh)

   (v.) to make a surprise attack from a hidden place
   A small force may try to _____ambush_____ *a larger one.*

   (n.) a surprise attack
   A famous _____ambush_____ *took place by that creek.*

   SYNONYMS: to attack, trap, waylay; a trap

2. **calculate**
   ('kal kyə lāt)

   (v.) to find out by adding, subtracting, multiplying, or dividing; to figure out by reason or logic
   Let's _____calculate_____ *the full cost of the class trip.*

   SYNONYMS: to compute, figure, reckon, evaluate
   ANTONYM: to estimate

3. **contribute**
   (kən 'tri byət)

   (v.) to give money, effort, or items for a cause; to hand in for publication
   Can you _____contribute_____ *some brownies to our bake sale?*

   SYNONYMS: to donate, offer, provide; to submit
   ANTONYM: to withhold

4. **dread**
   (dred)

   (v.) to be afraid; to fear or feel deep worry
   Many students _____dread_____ *surprise tests.*

   (n.) deep fear or uneasiness over what may happen
   A _____dread_____ *of talking in front of others keeps some students from raising their hands in class.*

   SYNONYMS: to fear; horror, terror
   ANTONYMS: to welcome, embrace; courage, excitement

5. **employ**
   (im 'ploi)

   (v.) to make use of; to put to work on a job or task for pay
   You may need to _____employ_____ *a compass in order to draw a perfect circle.*

   SYNONYMS: to use, hire, engage
   ANTONYM: to dismiss

6. **extend**
   (ik 'stend)

   (v.) to stretch out, make or last longer; to give or offer
   Let's _____extend_____ *our vacation into September.*

   SYNONYMS: to lengthen, increase, continue, enlarge; to grant
   ANTONYMS: to decrease, lessen, limit; to deny

30

Figure skaters must practice many hours every day in order to perfect the **routines** (word 9) they will perform in competition.

7. frantic
('fran tik)

(adj.) very excited or upset; marked by fast, wild, or nervous action
The scene ended with a _____frantic_____ search for the lost keys.

SYNONYMS: desperate, frenzied, distracted
ANTONYMS: calm, careful, orderly

8. initial
(i 'ni shəl)

(adj.) beginning or first
Our _____initial_____ reaction was anger.

(n.) the first letter of a name or word
I picked the _____initial_____ H for Hannah.

(v.) to mark or sign with one's initials
Please _____initial_____ all papers you correct.

SYNONYMS: first, earliest, opening
ANTONYMS: final, last

9. routine
(rü 'tēn)

(n.) the regular or fixed way in which a thing is done; an act or skit
The skaters practiced their _____routine_____.

(adj.) normal, predictable, or commonly done; repeated by habit
My _____routine_____ morning jog is three miles.

SYNONYMS: a pattern, procedure; ordinary, expected, typical, customary, usual
ANTONYMS: random, irregular, unusual

10. stun
(stən)

(v.) to have a sudden, upsetting effect on the mind or feelings; to shock or daze; to make unable to feel, react, or think
Bright lights may _____stun_____ a deer for a moment.

SYNONYMS: to astonish, bewilder, deaden, overwhelm, paralyze

11. sturdy
('stər dē)

(adj.) firmly or solidly built; determined
A police officer needs a pair of _____sturdy_____ shoes.

SYNONYMS: rugged, hardy, tough, powerful, durable
ANTONYMS: delicate, feeble, weak

12. yield
(yēld)

(v.) to give in or give way; to produce or bring forth
I was forced to _____yield_____ to her logic.

(n.) the product or amount made or produced
They got a good _____yield_____ from the pear trees.

SYNONYMS: to surrender, obey; a harvest, crop
ANTONYM: to resist

Match the Meaning

For each item below choose the word whose meaning is suggested by the clue given. Then write the word in the space provided.

1. To worry deeply over what may happen is to feel a sense of _____dread_____.
   a. yield   b. initial   c. dread   d. routine

2. Add columns of numbers to _____calculate_____ the sum.
   a. extend   b. calculate   c. employ   d. stun

3. Can you _____contribute_____ any books to our library?
   a. calculate   b. employ   c. contribute   d. stun

4. A surprise attack is a(n) _____ambush_____.
   a. ambush   b. dread   c. yield   d. routine

5. To be shocked is to be _____stunned_____.
   a. calculated   b. stunned   c. employed   d. extended

6. I must _____extend_____ my arm to reach the top shelf.
   a. dread   b. initial   c. ambush   d. extend

7. To give in to demands is to _____yield_____ to them.
   a. ambush   b. extend   c. stun   d. yield

8. The _____initial_____ score is the one that comes first.
   a. sturdy   b. routine   c. frantic   d. initial

9. The usual way you do things is your _____routine_____.
   a. routine   b. ambush   c. initial   d. yield

10. If I pay you to work for me, I _____employ_____ you.
    a. employ   b. calculate   c. ambush   d. extend

11. It takes a(n) _____sturdy_____ bike to handle rough mountain roads.
    a. sturdy   b. frantic   c. initial   d. routine

12. Someone who is very upset may be said to be _____frantic_____.
    a. frantic   b. initial   c. routine   d. sturdy

Synonyms

For each item below choose the word that is most nearly the **same** in meaning as the word or phrase in **boldface**. Then write your choice on the line provided.

1. **bewildered** by an angry reaction
   a. calculated   b. dreaded   c. stunned   d. extended   _____ stunned

2. **figure** the damage caused by the flood
   a. contribute   b. calculate   c. employ   d. stun   _____ calculate

3. lured into a **trap**
   a. dread   b. initial   c. ambush   d. routine   _____ ambush

4. lines that **continue** around the block
   a. ambush   b. dread   c. employ   d. extend   _____ extend

5. an **ordinary** inspection
   a. routine   b. initial   c. sturdy   d. frantic   _____ routine

6. **submit** your best photograph to the newspaper
   a. calculate   b. employ   c. dread   d. contribute   _____ contribute

Antonyms

For each item below choose the word that is most nearly **opposite** in meaning to the word or phrase in **boldface**. Then write your choice on the line provided.

1. a **calm** reply
   a. routine   b. initial   c. frantic   d. sturdy   _____ frantic

2. **dismiss** two new workers
   a. employ   b. ambush   c. stun   d. calculate   _____ employ

3. the **final** letter of her name
   a. initial   b. sturdy   c. frantic   d. routine   _____ initial

4. **welcome** a visit
   a. calculate   b. contribute   c. dread   d. employ   _____ dread

5. a **flimsy** fence
   a. frantic   b. initial   c. routine   d. sturdy   _____ sturdy

6. ordered them to **resist**
   a. contribute   b. dread   c. yield   d. employ   _____ yield

Completing the Sentence

From the list of words on pages 30–31, choose the one that best completes each item below. Then write the word in the space provided. (You may have to change the word's ending.)

FACING THE UNKNOWN

■ The pioneers who first traveled west carried all of their worldly goods in big, _____**sturdy**_____ wagons.

■ The normal evening _____**routine**_____ involved building a fire, cooking a meal, feeding the animals, making repairs to their wagons, and trying to get some rest.

■ Some pioneers feared deadly _____**ambushes**_____ by Native Americans who wanted to protect their lands.

■ Pioneers _____**dreaded**_____ bad weather, broken gear, and dangerous river crossings.

■ Weary travelers were _____**stunned**_____ by how small and rough some frontier settlements really were. For some, the shock was so great that they decided to turn around and return to the East.

■ Parents grew _____**frantic**_____ if children got sick, because medicine was scarce.

TIME FOR TIMES

■ "We begin a new unit today with our _____**initial**_____ lesson on multiplying," said the math teacher.

■ Students learned that 4 + 4 + 4 _____**yields**_____ the same answer as 3 × 4.

■ We can _____**calculate**_____ the basic facts of multiplication until we learn them by heart.

HOLIDAY KINDNESS

■ The holiday food drive _____**employs**_____ more than ten people. In addition to the people who are paid to organize and lead the drive, many others volunteer to help without any pay at all.

■ Workers take the canned goods that people _____**contribute**_____ and deliver them to needy families.

■ This year's food drive will be _____**extended**_____ for an extra week so more people can donate goods.

1. Soldiers might wait in **ambush** behind a
   a. shopping cart
   b. stop sign
   c. clump of trees
   d. swing set

2. Which would you **calculate**?
   a. sales tax
   b. lunch
   c. a vacation
   d. a bus

3. Which might **stun** you?
   a. a lullaby
   b. a blow to the head
   c. a funny cartoon
   d. a sneeze

4. Most people **dread** hearing
   a. children giggle
   b. birds sing
   c. the television
   d. terrible news

5. To **extend** a supply of paper,
   a. use both sides
   b. buy more pencils
   c. use one side only
   d. sharpen your scissors

6. All restaurants **employ**
   a. outfielders
   b. cooks
   c. judges
   d. dentists

7. The **initial** syllable in the word *supermarket* is
   a. *su*
   b. *per*
   c. *mar*
   d. *ket*

8. You might say I'm **frantic** if I'm
   a. relaxing on the couch
   b. watching television
   c. rushing around the room
   d. doing a crossword puzzle

9. To **contribute** to a good cause,
   a. give three hours of your time
   b. ask to get paid
   c. lock your door
   d. get a haircut

10. Soccer warm-up **routines** include
    a. mowing the grass
    b. shopping for new uniforms
    c. having a play-off game
    d. stretching arms and legs

11. Dairy cows will **yield**
    a. hay
    b. hens
    c. milk
    d. barns

12. Which shoes are most **sturdy**?
    a. flip-flop sandals
    b. hiking boots
    c. high-heeled pumps
    d. fuzzy slippers

Selecting Word Meanings

*For each of the following items circle the choice that is most nearly the **same** in meaning as the word in **boldface**.*

1. carried a great **burden**
   a. book
   b. sign
   c. treasure
   d. load

2. signed a new **contract**
   a. agreement
   b. check
   c. autograph
   d. letter

3. **stunned** by the bad news
   a. amused
   b. intrigued
   c. dazed
   d. annoyed

4. faced many **hardships**
   a. stampedes
   b. misfortunes
   c. challenges
   d. surprises

5. decided to **extend** our trip
   a. cancel
   b. delay
   c. plan
   d. lengthen

6. **calculate** the sale price
   a. ignore
   b. figure
   c. cancel
   d. pay

7. gave their **consent**
   a. permission
   b. answer
   c. greetings
   d. objections

8. a feeling of **dread**
   a. delight
   b. weakness
   c. fear
   d. responsibility

9. serve as our **counsel**
   a. guest
   b. lawyer
   c. leader
   d. representative

10. packed the books in a **sturdy** box
    a. flimsy
    b. empty
    c. large
    d. durable

11. **pledge** to tell the truth
    a. promise
    b. forget
    c. refuse
    d. remember

12. received an **attractive** offer
    a. sincere
    b. unusual
    c. inviting
    d. special

Spelling

For each item below study the **boldface** word in which there is a blank. If a letter is missing, fill in the blank to make a correctly spelled word. If the word is already spelled correctly, leave the blank empty.

1. a friendly **comp_e_tition**

2. **y_i_eld** to the majority

3. **spon_s_or** the event

4. **n_e_glect** the plants

5. **obtai__n** permission

6. **rout_i_ne** chores

7. learn **basi_c_** skills

8. **demonst_r_ate** the move

9. **e_m_ploy** an assistant

10. **su_i_table** behavior

11. **di_s_miss** the students

12. survived the **amb__ush**

Antonyms

For each of the following items circle the choice that is most nearly the **opposite** in meaning to the word in **boldface**.

1. their **initial** offer
   a. best   b. second   c. final   d. first

2. received a **portion**
   a. whole   b. serving   c. response   d. pledge

3. a **drowsy** audience
   a. noisy   b. tired   c. silent   d. alert

4. **sincere** thanks
   a. heartfelt   b. phony   c. unexpected   d. warm

5. that **vacant** house
   a. occupied   b. beautiful   c. expensive   d. run-down

6. read the **previous** chapter
   a. first   b. following   c. last   d. longest

7. a **stern** voice
   a. deep   b. loud   c. gentle   d. harsh

8. **frantic** crowds of shoppers
   a. tired   b. happy   c. angry   d. orderly

Vocabulary in Context

Words have been left out of the following passage. For each numbered item in the passage, fill in the circle next to the word in the margin that best fills the blank space. Then answer each question below by writing a sentence that contains one of the words you have chosen.

On April 11, 1970, a crew of three confident astronauts went into space on the Apollo 13 mission. There was nothing about the launch to __1__ that anything unexpected might happen. The astronauts were planning another historic walk on the Moon. They had trained for months to prepare for anything they might face during the mission. But no one predicted the __2__ situation they had to deal with when an oxygen tank exploded. This accident nearly crippled the spacecraft.

Of course the astronauts were worried. Their only hope was to stay calm and follow every command the ground crew gave. As highly skilled professionals, the astronauts kept focused on what they had to do. They used all their courage to hide any __3__ feelings when they spoke to Mission Control.

Mission Control experts worked round the clock to plan a rescue. They formed teams to find ways to fix the damaged spacecraft, protect the astronauts, and return them to Earth. Their quick __4__ kept the emergency from turning into a terrible disaster. On April 17, the astronauts splashed down in the Pacific Ocean. Their mission had not gone as planned, but the astronauts had come safely home.

1. ○ qualify
   ● indicate
   ○ recall
   ○ calculate

2. ○ humble
   ○ vacant
   ○ drowsy
   ● urgent

3. ○ suitable
   ○ stern
   ● frantic
   ○ initial

4. ● response
   ○ competition
   ○ yield
   ○ neglect

5. What was the most important thing about the ground crew's actions?

   Their **response** was quick.

6. How did conditions on Apollo 13 change after the explosion?

   The situation was **urgent** because the ship lost light, water, and electricity.

7. What kind of feelings did the courageous astronauts try to hide from the ground crew?

   They had **frantic** feelings.

8. Why was the crew of the Apollo 13 confident as they went into space?

   There was nothing about the launch to **indicate** that anything unexpected might happen.

 **Analogies**

In each of the following circle the letter for the item that best completes the comparison. Then explain the relationship on the lines provided. The first one has been done for you.

1. **annual** is to **yearly** as
   a. previous is to later
   b. weekly is to daily
   c. unpleasant is to attractive
   d. ordinary is to routine

Relationship: *"Annual" and "yearly" are synonyms/have the same meaning; "ordinary" and "routine" also have the same meaning.*

2. **worn** is to **shabby** as
   a. sturdy is to flimsy
   b. vacant is to empty
   c. fresh is to stale
   d. stern is to gentle

Relationship: *"Worn" and "shabby" have the same meaning; "vacant" and "empty" also have the same meaning.*

3. **essential** is to **unnecessary** as
   a. sincere is to false
   b drowsy is to tired
   c. vanity is to conceit
   d. promise is to pledge

Relationship: *"Essential" and "unnecessary" are opposites/antonyms; "sincere" and "false" are also opposites/antonyms.*

4. **heat** is to **thaw** as
   a. rain is to dry
   b. ice is to warm
   c. cold is to freeze
   d. snow is to burn

Relationship: *Heat would make something thaw; cold would make something freeze.*

Challenge: Make up your own

Write a comparison using the words in the box below. (Hint: There are three possible analogies.) Then write the relationship on the lines provided. One comparison has been completed for you.

ladder	essential	fish	robin
tuna	stair	hardship	basic
burden	rung	bird	step

Analogy: _____ robin _____ is to _____ bird _____ as _____ tuna _____ is to _____ fish _____.

Relationship: A robin is a type of bird. A tuna is a type of fish.

Analogy: _____ is to _____ as _____ is to _____.

Relationship: See Table of Contents.

Word Families

*The words in **boldface** in the sentences below are related to words introduced in Units 1–4. For example, the nouns calculations and contributions in item 1 are related to the verbs calculate and contribute (both in Unit 4). Based on your understanding of the unit words, circle the related word in **boldface** that best completes each sentence.*

demonstrate	attractive	sincere	indicate	vacant
neglect	qualify	consent	response	burden
urgent	contribute	competition	dreadful	extend
counsel	suitable	dependable	employ	calculate

1. The generous (**calculations**/**contributions**) helped us to buy a VCR for our class.

2. It is the job of a (**competitor**/**counselor**) to give useful advice.

3. The point of the (**demonstration**/**vacancy**) was to show support for the workers.

4. Baby-sitters known for their (**dependability**/**employment**) are very popular with the families in our town.

5. In many labs, scientists are testing the (**urgency**/**suitability**) of new medicines for treating the common cold.

6. Are you sure you are ready to accept the (**burdensome**/**neglectful**) duties of caring for a pet?

7. Brown leaves can be an (**attraction**/**indication**) that a plant is getting too much water.

8. Good writing skills are a key (**qualification**/**extension**) for many kinds of jobs.

9. The front page of the newspaper showed a photo of a (**dreadful**/**insincere**) accident.

10. The (**consenting**/**unresponsive**) audience sat in stony silence after each of the comic's bad jokes.

Word Games

Use the clue and the given letters to complete each word. Write the missing letters of the word in the appropriate boxes. Then use the circled letters and the drawing to answer the CHALLENGE question below.

1. A quiz show

C O M P (E) T I T (I) O N

2. You do this when you remember.

(R) E (C) A L L

3. To be fit for something

Q U A (L) I F (Y)

4. A weight or hardship

B U R D (E) N

5. Ragged or faded

S H A (B) B Y

6. The opposite of expand

C O N T R A C (T)

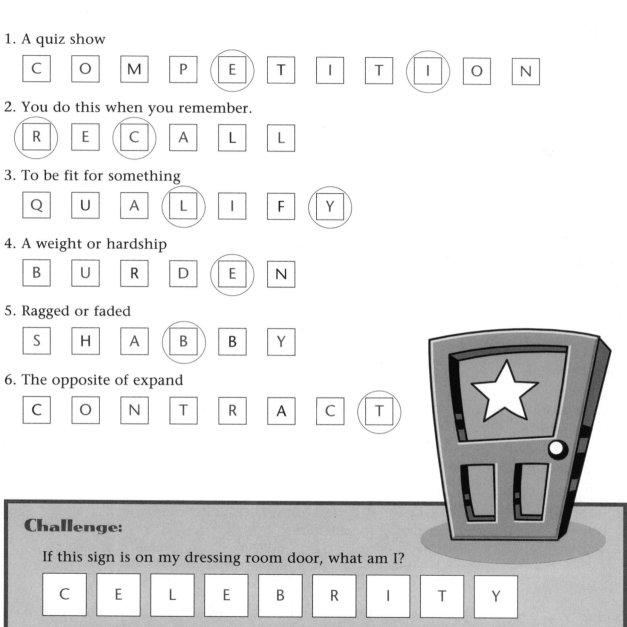

Challenge:

If this sign is on my dressing room door, what am I?

C E L E B R I T Y

UNIT 5

Definitions

Study the spelling, pronunciation, part of speech, and definition given for each of the words below. Write the word in the blank space in the sentence that follows. Then read the synonyms and antonyms.

1. **antique**
   (an 'tēk)

   (n.) an object made long ago; something made in the past
   Some people fill their homes with _____antiques_____.
   (adj.) from the past; very old
   The _____antique_____ cradle was carved in 1847.

   SYNONYMS: an heirloom, relic; ancient, old-fashioned, vintage
   ANTONYMS: modern, new, current, fresh

2. **baggage**
   ('ba gij)

   (n.) suitcases, bags, packages, equipment, or other items travelers carry; things that get in the way
   Many travelers carry too much _____baggage_____.

   SYNONYMS: luggage, trunks; a hindrance, burden, impediment

3. **digest**
   (n., 'dī jest;
   v., dī 'jest)

   (n.) a shortened version of previously published writings; a magazine that publishes such short versions
   My parents read a monthly _____digest_____ of international news.
   (v.) to understand or grasp an idea; to break down food within the body for nourishment; to make a short summary
   You may need time to _____digest_____ the lessons you learned in school this week.

   SYNONYMS: a summary; to absorb, assimilate, eat, consume, condense, summarize
   ANTONYMS: an extension, expansion; to enlarge, expand; to misunderstand

4. **establish**
   (is 'ta blish)

   (v.) to set up, start, organize, or bring about; to prove beyond doubt
   The new baby's parents will _____establish_____ a fund for her college education.

   SYNONYMS: to build, create, form, plant; to confirm, demonstrate, show
   ANTONYMS: to destroy, ruin; to disprove

5. **eternal**
   (i 'tər nəl)

   (adj.) lasting for all time; with no beginning or end; continuing forever; seeming to be endless
   Poets write of the _____eternal_____ promise of spring.

   SYNONYMS: everlasting; timeless; constant, permanent; continual
   ANTONYMS: temporary, ending; brief, fleeting, short; changeable

6. **haste**
   (hāst)

   (n.) speed or quickness of motion; overeager action without caution
   If you work in _____haste_____, you may make careless mistakes.

   SYNONYMS: hurry, swiftness; rashness, carelessness, recklessness
   ANTONYMS: slowness, delay; caution

Aviation **pioneers** (word 10) Orville and Wilbur Wright were the first to achieve controlled, powered flight and to build a practical airplane.

7. humid
('hyü məd)

(adj.) steamy or heavy with moisture; moist or damp
Icy lemonade is a refreshing treat on a _____ humid _____ *day.*
SYNONYMS: muggy, soggy, sweltering; wet, clammy
ANTONYMS: dry, arid

8. lash
(lash)

(v.) to whip or strike; to scold; to strap down with rope or cord
A cornered animal may _____ lash _____ *out in fear.*
(n.) a whip; a blow made by or as if by a whip; an eyelash
The man bore scars from the cruel _____ lash _____.
SYNONYMS: to flog, wave, thrash, hit; to tie, secure, fasten; to criticize, abuse
ANTONYMS: to caress, pat; to untie; to compliment, praise

9. oppose
(ə 'pōz)

(v.) to act or speak out against, resist, object to; to be in direct contrast with
A group of senators will _____ oppose _____ *the bill.*
SYNONYMS: to protest, fight, dispute, confront; to deny, combat, contradict
ANTONYMS: to aid, assist, approve, confirm, cooperate, favor, help, support, join

10. pioneer
(pī ə 'nir)

(n.) a person or group that goes first to explore, open, prepare, or settle an area; someone who breaks new ground, as in science or ideas
Jacques Cousteau was a _____ pioneer _____ *in exploring the ocean's depths.*
(v.) to open the way for others to follow; to lead, be the first
Our city will _____ pioneer _____ *the use of electric buses.*

11. sensible
('sen sə bəl)

(adj.) showing or having good judgment or reason; aware of
It's only _____ sensible _____ *to wear a warm coat on a cold day.*
SYNONYMS: reasonable, wise, prudent; informed, conscious, observant
ANTONYMS: foolish, unwise, unreasonable; unaware

12. worthy
('wər thē)

(adj.) having value, importance, or worth; good enough for
Many people volunteer to work for a _____ worthy _____ *charity.*
SYNONYMS: deserving, excellent, good, admirable, useful
ANTONYMS: worthless, unworthy, useless

Match the Meaning

For each item below choose the word whose meaning is suggested by the clue given. Then write the word in the space provided.

1. A person who starts a new business _____**establishes**_____ it.
   a. lashes   b. opposes   c. digests   d. establishes

2. If you chew your food well, it will be easier to _____**digest**_____.
   a. lash   b. digest   c. establish   d. pioneer

3. When you speak out against something, you _____**oppose**_____ it.
   a. digest   b. pioneer   c. oppose   d. establish

4. A table that is two hundred years old may be said to be a(n) _____**antique**_____.
   a. antique   b. baggage   c. digest   d. pioneer

5. Something that lasts forever is _____**eternal**_____.
   a. sensible   b. humid   c. worthy   d. eternal

6. The first person to walk on the Moon could be called a space _____**pioneer**_____.
   a. digest   b. pioneer   c. baggage   d. antique

7. A(n) _____**sensible**_____ person shows good judgment and awareness.
   a. sensible   b. eternal   c. pioneer   d. humid

8. The suitcases that I take with me when I go on a trip are my _____**baggage**_____.
   a. antiques   b. haste   c. baggage   d. lashes

9. If a magazine buys your poem, the editors must think it is _____**worthy**_____ of publication.
   a. humid   b. worthy   c. sensible   d. eternal

10. _____**Humid**_____ weather is steamy and damp.
    a. Antique   b. Eternal   c. Sensible   d. Humid

11. In an emergency it may be important to act in _____**haste**_____.
    a. pioneer   b. lash   c. haste   d. antique

12. When someone scolds you, they may be said to _____**lash**_____ you with words.
    a. lash   b. establish   c. digest   d. pioneer

Synonyms

*For each item below choose the word that is most nearly the **same** in meaning as the word or phrase in **boldface**. Then write your choice on the line provided.*

1. lit a **permanent** flame at the monument
   a. worthy   b. sensible   c. humid   d. eternal   _____ eternal _____

2. weighed down by heavy **packages**
   a. antiques   b. digests   c. pioneers   d. baggage   _____ baggage _____

3. **whipped** the prisoner
   a. lashed   b. pioneered   c. opposed   d. established   _____ lashed _____

4. **absorbed** the meaning of the speech
   a. opposed   b. digested   c. established   d. pioneered   _____ digested _____

5. clues that may **confirm** who did it
   a. digest   b. lash   c. establish   d. oppose   _____ establish _____

6. worked for **deserving** causes
   a. worthy   b. humid   c. antique   d. eternal   _____ worthy _____

Antonyms

*For each item below choose the word that is most nearly **opposite** in meaning to the word or phrase in **boldface**. Then write your choice on the line provided.*

1. a very **unwise** decision
   a. eternal   b. worthy   c. humid   d. sensible   _____ sensible _____

2. **supported** the candidate
   a. pioneered   b. opposed   c. lashed   d. established   _____ opposed _____

3. a set of **new** dishes
   a. antique   b. worthy   c. pioneer   d. sensible   _____ antique _____

4. a **dry** climate
   a. eternal   b. worthy   c. humid   d. sensible   _____ humid _____

5. an eager **follower**
   a. pioneer   b. antique   c. digest   d. lash   _____ pioneer _____

6. moved with **caution**
   a. baggage   b. pioneers   c. lashes   d. haste   _____ haste _____

Completing the Sentence

From the list of words on pages 42–43, choose the one that best completes each item below. Write the word in the space provided. (You may have to change the word's ending.)

TIPS FOR HIKERS

■ My friends and I love to hike, even on hot, sticky days. An experienced hiker gave us tips for staying comfortable in such _____**humid**_____ weather.

■ To begin with, _____**establish**_____ a plan and stick to it. Don't waste your energy.

■ Wear hats and sunscreen, drink lots of fluids, and never move in _____**haste**_____. Take your time; and always stop to rest when you feel tired.

A BIG STEP

■ I think of my great grandfather as a _____**pioneer**_____ because he was the first person from his tiny village to come to America.

■ At first his parents _____**opposed**_____ his decision. They worried about what would happen to him in a country where he knew no one and could not speak the language.

■ Finally he convinced them that seeking a better life was a _____**worthy**_____ and admirable goal in spite of the risks and uncertainties.

■ Grandfather filled his _____**baggage**_____ with clothes and tools. All of the belongings he would take with him he fit into two large trunks.

■ He _____**lashed**_____ his favorite books together with a leather strap and hung it over his shoulder.

■ Then he tucked his _____**antique**_____ watch safely in his pocket, said his good-byes, and started on his journey.

GOOD ADVICE

■ Like all living creatures, people have an _____**eternal**_____ need for nourishment.

■ When we _____**digest**_____ our food, our bodies turn it into the energy that keeps us going.

■ Doctors offer this very _____**sensible**_____ advice: Eat a variety of healthy foods, avoid too much sugar and fat, and drink lots of water.

Circle the letter next to the word or expression that best completes the sentence or answers the question. Pay special attention to the word in **boldface**.

1. To be **worthy** of the lead in the play, you should
   a. know how to sew costumes
   b. have a clear speaking voice
   c. be good in science and math
   d. have perfect attendance

2. Something **eternal** would
   a. last a while
   b. stop suddenly
   c. last forever
   d. stop before it starts

3. A **sensible** pet for an apartment
   a is a Shetland pony
   b. is a seal
   c. is a St. Bernard dog
   d. is a hamster

4. The **baggage** for my trip holds
   a. my hotel room
   b. my airplane seat
   c. my bathtub
   d. my pajamas

5. Most **pioneers** would wonder
   a. how to survive in a new area
   b. when to phone home
   c. where to get good pizza
   d. what time it is

6. Which of these is an **antique**?
   a. a cellular phone
   b. a Civil War sword
   c. a CD player
   d. a new car

7. To **establish** a good relationship, neighbors might
   a. play loud music late at night
   b. ruin each other's gardens
   c. break each other's windows
   d. smile and say hello

8. If someone **lashes** out at you,
   a. they scold you severely
   b. they ask you for directions
   c. they give you a gift
   d. they drive you to the mall

9. A science **digest** might print a
   a. recipe for lasagna
   b. long science-fiction novel
   c. summary of a medical study
   d. complete play about Dr. Seuss

10. To **oppose** closing the old library,
    a. speak out in public to save it
    b. return your overdue books
    c. get a wrecking ball
    d. move to another town

11. In a **humid** place, you might
    a. have a garage
    b. have damp towels
    c. have a credit card
    d. have a picnic

12. Which animal often moves in **haste**?
    a. a snail
    b. a turtle
    c. a rabbit
    d. a sloth

UNIT 6

Definitions

Study the spelling, pronunciation, part of speech, and definition given for each of the words below. Write the word in the blank space in the sentence that follows. Then read the synonyms and antonyms.

1. **blossom**
('blä səm)

(n.) a flower or group of flowers; the state or time of flowering
   *A rose garden in _____ **blossom** _____ sweetens the air.*
(v.) to have or produce flowers; to develop, open up, or appear
   *Steady encouragement can help a person's talent to _____ **blossom** _____.*
SYNONYMS: a bloom, bud; to unfold, flourish, grow
ANTONYMS: to shrink, wither, fade

2. **collide**
(kə 'līd)

(v.) to bump into hard, come together with force; to clash
   *Small meteors sometimes _____ **collide** _____ with the Moon.*
SYNONYMS: to crash, smash, hit, slam; to conflict
ANTONYMS: to avoid, evade, elude; to agree, consent, settle

3. **constant**
('kän stənt)

(adj.) never stopping; happening over and over again; staying the same; loyal, steady, or faithful
   *City dwellers get used to the _____ **constant** _____ hum of traffic.*
(n.) something that does not change or vary
   *The need for food is a _____ **constant** _____ for all living things.*
SYNONYMS: continuous, unchanging, endless, regular, uninterrupted; true, trusty
ANTONYMS: variable, changeable, irregular, random; faithless, fickle

4. **content**
(*adj.,* kən 'tent;
n., 'kän tent)

(adj.) pleased with or accepting of; not wanting anything else
   *Our neighbors are _____ **content** _____ with their new home.*
(n.) an amount that is held or contained; the meaning or subject of
   *The _____ **content** _____ of that book is too technical for me.*
SYNONYMS: satisfied, comfortable, fulfilled; the gist, theme
ANTONYMS: dissatisfied, unhappy, restless; discontent

5. **distract**
(di 'strakt)

(v.) to draw attention to something else or cause to turn aside; to confuse or disturb
   *Try not to let the noise _____ **distract** _____ you.*
SYNONYMS: to divert, sidetrack, interfere; to disturb, bother, interrupt
ANTONYMS: to focus, explain, concentrate

6. **drought**
(draut)

(n.) a long time without rain; a prolonged shortage
   *Farmers lost their entire crops because of the _____ **drought** _____.*
SYNONYMS: dryness; lack
ANTONYMS: a drenching, flood; a surplus, glut

7. **foul**
('faůl')

(adj.) unpleasant to the senses; dirty, clogged, or polluted; dishonorable; against the rules of a sport or game; stormy or rainy
The criminal was responsible for many _____**foul**_____ *deeds.*

(n.) a violation of the rules; a ball that goes outside boundary lines
The umpire ruled that the ball was a _____**foul**_____.

(v.) to pollute or make filthy; to break the rules of a game; to hit a foul
Leaky oil tanks can _____**foul**_____ *water and soil.*

SYNONYMS: offensive, nasty, smelly; a violation; to soil, contaminate
ANTONYMS: attractive, clean, clear, fair, honest, pleasant, pure; to clean, purify

8. **noble**
('no bəl)

(adj.) of high birth or rank; outstanding, of good moral character
The hero of the play is a _____**noble**_____ *lord.*

(n.) someone of high rank or birth
A commoner may gain a title by marrying a _____**noble**_____.

SYNONYMS: highborn; honorable; lofty, splendid, majestic; an aristocrat
ANTONYMS: base, ignoble, lowly; a commoner

9. **policy**
('pä lə sē)

(n.) a plan, set of rules, or way to act; a written insurance contract
The store changed its refund _____**policy**_____.

SYNONYMS: guidelines, procedures; a code, system, practice

10. **quiver**
('kwi vər)

(n.) a case used to hold arrows; a trembling or shaking motion
Only one arrow was left in the archer's _____**quiver**_____.

(v.) to shake or tremble
When I am nervous, my hands _____**quiver**_____.

SYNONYMS: a sheath; a tremor, shiver; to tremble, shudder, flutter, quake, vibrate

11. **slight**
(slīt)

(adj.) small in size or degree; not much; not important
There may be _____**slight**_____ *delays in train service.*

(v.) to treat as unimportant; to make light of
A good host and hostess never _____**slight**_____ *their guests.*

(n.) an act of neglect or discourtesy
I apologized for the unintentional _____**slight**_____.

SYNONYMS: slender, minor, trivial; to neglect, snub; an insult
ANTONYMS: husky, muscular, large, strong; important, major; a compliment

12. **tidy**
('tī dē)

(adj.) neat and in good order; comfortable or large in amount
I was surprised to receive a _____**tidy**_____ *reward.*

(v.) to put things in neat or proper order
Be sure to _____**tidy**_____ *the room before you go.*

SYNONYMS: orderly, clean, trim; generous, large, substantial; to neaten, organize
ANTONYMS: messy, disordered, dirty, sloppy; small; to litter, jumble, clutter, confuse

Match the Meaning

For each item below choose the word whose meaning is suggested by the clue given. Then write the word in the space provided.

1. Something that takes your attention away from your homework may be said to _____**distract**_____ you.
   a. collide   b. quiver   c. slight   d. distract

2. When the cherry trees _____**blossom**_____ it is a sure sign of spring.
   a. distract   b. blossom   c. quiver   d. collide

3. To shake is to _____**quiver**_____.
   a. slight   b. distract   c. quiver   d. distract

4. A guide dog is the blind person's _____**constant**_____ partner.
   a. constant   b. content   c. foul   d. tidy

5. If your closet is neat and organized, it is _____**tidy**_____.
   a. slight   b. noble   c. foul   d. tidy

6. Stormy weather may be described as _____**foul**_____.
   a. constant   b. foul   c. noble   d. slight

7. A _____**slight**_____ is an act of discourtesy.
   a. slight   b. blossom   c. foul   d. noble

8. A long period of time without rain is called a _____**drought**_____.
   a. constant   b. policy   c. drought   d. quiver

9. When skaters _____**collide**_____, they bump into each other with force.
   a. blossom   b. collide   c. distract   d. quiver

10. A person of good moral character may perform _____**noble**_____ acts.
    a. constant   b. tidy   c. slight   d. noble

11. Rules on how to act on the job form the company's _____**policy**_____ for workers.
    a. blossom   b. content   c. policy   d. drought

12. People who are _____**content**_____ with their lives feel happy and satisfied.
    a. content   b. constant   c. slight   d. noble

Synonyms

*For each item below choose the word that is most nearly the **same** in meaning as the word or phrase in **boldface**. Then write your choice on the line provided.*

1. flowers that **flutter** in the breeze
   a. quiver   b. blossom   c. distract   d. collide   **quiver**

2. a **highborn** family
   a. tidy   b. content   c. noble   d. slight   **noble**

3. **contaminate** the water supply
   a. slight   b. quiver   c. distract   d. foul   **foul**

4. saw the players **crash**
   a. collide   b. blossom   c. distract   d. quiver   **collide**

5. the **theme** of the story
   a. slight   b. content   c. policy   d. quiver   **content**

6. an insurance **contract**
   a. drought   b. constant   c. policy   d. blossom   **policy**

Antonyms

*For each item below choose the word that is most nearly **opposite** in meaning to the word or phrase in **boldface**. Then write your choice on the line provided.*

1. **withers** on the vine
   a. collides   b. blossoms   c. quivers   d. distracts   **blossoms**

2. a **messy** room
   a. foul   b. slight   c. tidy   d. noble   **tidy**

3. an unexpected **compliment**
   a. blossom   b. quiver   c. policy   d. slight   **slight**

4. **focus** the students' attention
   a. collide   b. slight   c. distract   d. blossom   **distract**

5. a **flood** of good ideas
   a. slight   b. quiver   c. policy   d. drought   **drought**

6. a **fickle** friend
   a. tidy   b. constant   c. noble   d. slight   **constant**

Completing the Sentence

From the list of words on pages 48–49, choose the one that best completes each item below. Write the word in the space provided. (You may have to change the word's ending.)

DRY TIMES

■ Last year there was almost no rain in our state. No one knew how long the _____ **drought** _____ would last.

■ For many months the weather was unusually hot. The _____ **constant** _____ heat dried up fields and gardens.

■ Withered leaves and plants _____ **quivered** _____ in the hot breezes. It was a sad sight.

■ Many farmers lost their crops. Apple growers were especially hard hit. Most of their trees did not _____ **blossom** _____. When it was time for the harvest, there were only a few apples to pick.

AN UNPLEASANT TASK

■ Everyone in my family has a regular household job to do. Mine is keeping the refrigerator clean and _____ **tidy** _____.

■ I am supposed to check the _____ **contents** _____ of the refrigerator once a week. But last week I forgot to do it.

■ My mom was very annoyed. She asked me to make the "_____ **noble** _____" effort to clean up the mess.

■ A _____ **foul** _____ odor hit my nose when I opened the door. What was that disgusting thing at the back of the shelf? My science project? No, it was just a moldy sandwich that I forgot to take to school.

SAFETY IN THE PARK

■ Everyone enjoys our city park. That means the park can get very crowded, especially on weekends. All that activity can _____ **distract** _____ people, and quite a few have been hurt.

■ To cut down on the number of accidents, the mayor has put a park safety _____ **policy** _____ into effect.

■ Skaters and bicycle riders are required to slow down when they get near a crosswalk. This rule is intended to keep them from _____ **colliding** _____ with people who are trying to get to the other side of the road.

■ If people follow the rules and stay alert, their chances of being injured are _____ **slight** _____.

Word Associations — *Circle the letter next to the word or expression that best completes the sentence or answers the question. Pay special attention to the word in **boldface**.*

1. When two baseball players **collide**, they
   a. shake hands
   b. tell jokes
   c. crash into each other
   d. sing the national anthem

2. You can **tidy** up the kitchen by
   a. having a dinner party
   b. watering the plants
   c. opening the windows
   d. washing the dirty dishes

3. Which might develop a **blossom**?
   a. a lightbulb
   b. a magnolia tree
   c. a cup of tea
   d. a baseball glove

4. During a **drought** you will see
   a. wilted plants
   b. open umbrellas
   c. green lawns
   d. deep puddles

5. A **quivering** puppy might be
   a. sleepy
   b. cold
   c. running
   d. growing

6. If I walk at a **constant** rate,
   a. I won't cross the street
   b. I won't get lost
   c. I won't go faster or slower
   d. I won't get thirsty

7. If something **distracts** me, it
   a. gives me a toothache
   b. interrupts my thoughts
   c. makes me hungry
   d. helps me to study

8. If I am **content** with my homework, I
   a. lose it
   b. do it over
   c. read it out loud
   d. hand it in

9. A **noble** might live in a
   a. palace
   b. tent
   c. homeless shelter
   d. houseboat

10. When a ball is **foul**, it
    a. breaks a window
    b. goes into the goal
    c. goes out of bounds
    d. doesn't bounce

11. To **slight** your cousins, you might
    a. ignore them
    b. grow taller than they are
    c. hug them
    d. bring them gifts

12. Which of these is a **policy**?
    a. a menu
    b. a timetable
    c. a movie ticket
    d. a dress code

Unit 6 ■ 53

Definitions

Study the spelling, pronunciation, part of speech, and definition given for each of the words below. Write the word in the blank space in the sentence that follows. Then read the synonyms and antonyms.

1. **accurate**
   ('a kyə rət)

   (adj.) without errors, completely correct; conforming to the truth
   It is important to take _____ accurate _____ notes in class.

   SYNONYMS: exact, precise; true, careful
   ANTONYMS: mistaken, wrong, false, questionable, misleading; inaccurate, careless

2. **alert**
   (ə 'lərt)

   (adj.) watchful and ready to act; quick to understand and act
   A good watchdog is _____ alert _____ and protective.

   (n.) readiness; an alarm; a time when an alarm is in effect
   Police and firefighters are always on _____ alert _____.

   (v.) to warn or make aware of
   Signs on a highway _____ alert _____ drivers of hazards.

   SYNONYMS: attentive, vigilant; a signal; to notify, inform
   ANTONYMS: inattentive, unobservant, unaware

3. **ancestor**
   ('an ses tər)

   (n.) a family member who lived at an earlier time
   You may want to study the lives of your _____ ancestors _____.

   SYNONYMS: a forerunner, forebear, forefather, foremother
   ANTONYM: a descendant

4. **disaster**
   (di 'zas tər)

   (n.) a sudden, terrible event that brings great damage or suffering; a great failure
   It took months to recover from the _____ disaster _____.

   SYNONYMS: a tragedy, catastrophe, calamity, misfortune, trouble
   ANTONYMS: a success, triumph

5. **elementary**
   (e lə 'men tə rē)

   (adj.) related to the simplest or beginning level of something
   Beginning students of the piano practice _____ elementary _____ pieces to develop their skills.

   SYNONYMS: basic, beginning, fundamental, introductory
   ANTONYMS: complex, hard, difficult, advanced

6. **envy**
   ('en vē)

   (n.) a feeling of resentment caused by longing for what someone has; a person or object that is envied
   Our team's winning season was the _____ envy _____ of the league.

   (v.) to resent and want what someone else has
   There may be times when you _____ envy _____ another person's good luck in life.

   SYNONYMS: jealousy, desire, greed; to covet, begrudge
   ANTONYM: satisfaction

7. **epidemic**
(e pə 'de mik)

(adj.) spreading to a very large group at the same time; contagious
Polio was once _____ epidemic _____ in the United States.

(n.) a rapid and widespread outbreak of a disease; sudden rapid growth or development
An _____ epidemic _____ of Dutch elm disease destroyed hundreds of trees in our town park.

SYNONYMS: catching, infectious; rife, widespread, universal; an infection, plague
ANTONYMS: isolated, contained, limited

8. **feeble**
('fē bəl)

(adj.) having little strength or force; without energy or authority
The exhausted runner managed to give us a _____ feeble _____ smile after the long race.

SYNONYMS: weak, frail, faint, fragile
ANTONYMS: able, strong, forceful, powerful; energetic

9. **penetrate**
('pe nə trāt)

(v.) to enter or force a way through or into; to see into
Cars are equipped with special lights that can _____ penetrate _____ fog.

SYNONYMS: to pass through, pierce, puncture; to see; to grasp, realize
ANTONYMS: to withdraw; to misunderstand

10. **romp**
(rämp)

(n.) spirited, carefree, or noisy fun; something that suggests merry play
The class enjoyed a _____ romp _____ in the playground.

(v.) to run or play in a lively or carefree way; to win easily
We watched the puppies _____ romp _____ on the lawn.

SYNONYMS: a lark, frolic, sport, caper; to caper, frolic, skip, bound

11. **staple**
('stā pəl)

(n.) a U-shaped wire that fastens material by piercing and bending; a major product, material, part, or item regularly used
Fruits and vegetables are _____ staples _____ of a healthy diet.

(v.) to fasten with staples
Please _____ staple _____ the pages of your report together.

(adj.) chief, principal; needed or used regularly
Rice is a _____ staple _____ crop in many Asian countries.

SYNONYMS: necessities; basics; basic, main, important, essential
ANTONYMS: nonessentials; minor, unnecessary

12. **survive**
(sər 'vīv)

(v.) to stay alive or continue to exist; to keep on going; to live longer than
We need food and shelter in order to _____ survive _____.

SYNONYMS: to live, persist; to endure, last, withstand; to outlive
ANTONYMS: to die, perish

Match the Meaning

For each item below choose the word whose meaning is suggested by the clue given. Then write the word in the space provided.

1. If a team wins a game easily, it may be said to _____**romp**_____ over its opponents.
   a. survive   b. penetrate   c. envy   d. romp

2. If I wish I had the advantages that someone else enjoys, I _____**envy**_____ that person.
   a. alert   b. envy   c. survive   d. staple

3. To pierce or enter something is to _____**penetrate**_____ it.
   a. alert   b. survive   c. penetrate   d. envy

4. A widespread outbreak of a disease is called an _____**epidemic**_____.
   a. epidemic   b. alert   c. envy   d. ancestor

5. The _____**elementary**_____ lessons are the easiest ones.
   a. accurate   b. feeble   c. staple   d. elementary

6. The major product produced in a state may be called a(n) _____**staple**_____.
   a. alert   b. staple   c. disaster   d. epidemic

7. A(n) _____**accurate**_____ watch shows the exact time.
   a. accurate   b. elementary   c. alert   d. feeble

8. Members of your family who lived in the distant past are called your _____**ancestors**_____.
   a. epidemics   b. disasters   c. ancestors   d. romps

9. If you stay alive or keep going, you _____**survive**_____.
   a. envy   b. survive   c. romp   d. penetrate

10. An action that lacks strength and authority is a(n) _____**feeble**_____ effort.
    a. accurate   b. elementary   c. staple   d. feeble

11. A severe storm that causes great property damage is a natural _____**disaster**_____.
    a. envy   b. romp   c. disaster   d. ancestor

12. If I am _____**alert**_____, I am watchful and ready for whatever happens.
    a. alert   b. feeble   c. accurate   d. elementary

Synonyms

*For each item below choose the word that is most nearly the **same** in meaning as the word or phrase in **boldface**. Then write your choice on the line provided.*

1. an **introductory** class in astronomy
   a. accurate   b. epidemic   c. feeble   d. elementary   _____ elementary _____

2. a **plague** of unknown cause
   a. alert   b. epidemic   c. ancestor   d. romp   _____ epidemic _____

3. **passed through** enemy lines
   a. penetrated   b. envied   c. alerted   d. survived   _____ penetrated _____

4. **covets** the prize
   a. penetrates   b. envies   c. survives   d. staples   _____ envies _____

5. **skipped** along
   a. survived   b. alerted   c. romped   d. penetrated   _____ romped _____

6. financial **catastrophes**
   a. ancestors   b. romps   c. staples   d. disasters   _____ disasters _____

Antonyms

*For each item below choose the word that is most nearly **opposite** in meaning to the word or phrase in **boldface**. Then write your choice on the line provided.*

1. not expected to **die**
   a. romp   b. survive   c. envy   d. penetrate   _____ survive _____

2. **misleading** information about the law
   a. alert   b. elementary   c. feeble   d. accurate   _____ accurate _____

3. made a **strong** effort
   a. accurate   b. feeble   c. alert   d. elementary   _____ feeble _____

4. an **inattentive** audience
   a. alert   b. staple   c. accurate   d. feeble   _____ alert _____

5. bought many **unnecessary** items
   a. feeble   b. alert   c. staple   d. accurate   _____ staple _____

6. **descendants** of the pioneers
   a. ancestors   b. disasters   c. epidemics   d. staples   _____ ancestors _____

From the list of words on pages 54–55, choose the one that best completes each item below. Write the word in the space provided. (You may have to change the word's ending.)

THE QUICKNESS OF SICKNESS

■ News reports predicted that this winter's flu _____**epidemic**_____ would be very bad.

■ Our state's health department tried to _____**alert**_____ people to the importance of getting their flu shots as early as possible. Unfortunately the disease spread so quickly that many people did not have a chance to protect themselves.

■ The symptoms of this year's strain of flu left even strong people _____**feeble**_____ and unable to take care of themselves.

MUSIC AND LEARNING

■ Music can be an important teaching tool in the _____**elementary**_____ school classroom.

■ Singing and movement are recognized as _____**staples**_____ of young children's learning, almost as essential as reading and arithmetic.

■ Songs can help children to remember such things as the alphabet. Musical games that involve movement may be a(n) _____**romp**_____ for the youngsters. But they also help children to develop good physical coordination.

■ Learning to play a simple instrument can help children to develop a(n) _____**accurate**_____ sense of rhythm and to learn to count.

NO WARNING

■ The story of my mother's _____**ancestors**_____ is dramatic. They settled in the Pennsylvania city of Johnstown in the early 1800s.

■ They did well in business and lived comfortably. According to family legend, their beautiful house was the _____**envy**_____ of their neighbors for decades. But in an instant, all of that changed.

■ On May 31, 1889, a terrible _____**disaster**_____ struck Johnstown. A dam collapsed, sending a deadly flood through the city.

■ When rescue workers were able to _____**penetrate**_____ the wreckage, they found terrible destruction. More than two thousand people had been killed, and the damage to property was widespread.

■ My mother's family was more fortunate than many. They lost all their material possessions, but they _____**survived**_____. They knew that as long as they were together, they could rebuild their lives.

Word Associations

*Circle the letter next to the word or expression that best completes the sentence or answers the question. Pay special attention to the word in **boldface**.*

1. If my math homework is **accurate**, I have made
   a. many mistakes
   b. several mistakes
   c. two mistakes
   d. no mistakes

2. In **elementary** school you find
   a. kindergarten students
   b. college students
   c. twelfth graders
   d. eighth graders

3. Plants that **survive** the winter
   a. are delicate
   b. are sturdy
   c. are flowery
   d. are dead

4. Tools that **penetrate** wood must
   a. be expensive
   b. be new
   c. be sharp
   d. be curved

5. During an **epidemic**, you might
   a. catch chicken pox
   b. become a doctor
   c. get very hungry
   d. go to the mall

6. Your neighbors may **envy** your
   a. broken windows
   b. rusty old car
   c. beautiful lawn
   d. crabgrass

7. Which of these **alerts** you in case of fire?
   a. a smoke detector
   b. an alarm clock
   c. a personal stereo
   d. an E-mail message

8. Which is a **disaster**?
   a. an earthworm
   b. an earthling
   c. an earthmover
   d. an earthquake

9. A **staple** product of Hawaii is
   a. pinecones
   b. pineapples
   c. pumpkins
   d. pizza

10. A mammoth is whose **ancestor**?
   a. the chipmunk
   b. the cave dwellers
   c. your grandparents
   d. the elephant

11. A **feeble** argument would
   a. not convince anybody
   b. cause a war
   c. last for a few weeks
   d. involve lots of yelling

12. Who is probably having a **romp**?
   a. a man working in a library
   b. a boy sitting and weeping
   c. a girl doing cartwheels
   d. a woman driving a truck

Definitions

Study the spelling, pronunciation, part of speech, and definition given for each of the words below. Write the word in the blank space in the sentence that follows. Then read the synonyms and antonyms.

1. **awkward**
('ô kwərd)

(adj.) not skillful or graceful; hard to handle; embarrassing
When you first learn to dance, your movements may be ____awkward____.
SYNONYMS: clumsy, ungainly, bumbling, inept, unskilled; difficult, unmanageable
ANTONYMS: graceful, skillful, pleasant, handy; manageable

2. **clatter**
('kla tər)

(v.) to make short, sharp sounds by rattling or banging together; to speak or move with confused, noisy sound
The old trains ____clatter____ as they move down the tracks.
(n.) a hard, rattling sound; busy excitement; noisy chattering
The ____clatter____ of machines in some factories is extremely loud.
SYNONYMS: to rattle, chatter; a racket, commotion

3. **gallant**
(*n.*, gə 'lant;
adj., 'ga lənt)

(adj.) showy in appearance; splendid; brave or full of spirit, showing courtesy; very attentive
We saw the parade of ____gallant____ sailing ships.
(n.) a fashionable young gentleman; a suitor
The heroine of the novel was courted by a wealthy ____gallant____.
SYNONYMS: splendid, dashing; valiant, heroic, daring; polite, considerate, chivalrous
ANTONYMS: afraid, cowardly, timid; selfish, rude; a slob, hobo

4. **lukewarm**
('lük wôrm)

(adj.) only moderately warm, not hot but not cold; without enthusiasm
A dull speech is likely to get ____lukewarm____ applause.
SYNONYMS: tepid, halfhearted
ANTONYMS: steaming hot, boiling; icy, freezing; eager, enthusiastic

5. **plentiful**
('plen ti fəl)

(adj.) in great supply, easily available; more than enough
Flowers are ____plentiful____ in springtime.
SYNONYMS: ample, abundant, bountiful
ANTONYMS: scarce, rare, meager

6. **ration**
('ra shən)

(n.) a portion of food allowed for one meal or one day; food or supplies; a share
A soup kitchen provides ____rations____ to the poor.
(v.) to pass out in limited portions; to limit the use of
When water is scarce, people must ____ration____ it.
SYNONYMS: an allowance, share, allotment; provisions; to parcel, divide, dispense

7. reserve
(ri 'zərv)

(v.) to hold back or set aside; to save for future use
Please _____ **reserve** _____ *a seat for me.*

(n.) something set aside for a certain purpose; something stored for later use; the use of care or caution in actions or words
We watched the squirrel dig up its _____ **reserve** _____ *of nuts.*

SYNONYMS: to store, retain, stash, withhold; a supply, stock; restraint, composure
ANTONYMS: to splurge, squander, waste, use; boldness, warmth

8. scholar
('skä lər)

(n.) a learned person; an expert in a field of study; someone who studies with a teacher; a student who gets a gift of money to pay for education
The book was written by a respected _____ **scholar** _____.

SYNONYMS: a sage, professor, authority, pupil

9. smolder
('smol dər)

(v.) to burn slowly, with smoke but no flame; to exist in a suppressed state; to show suppressed feelings
A person may _____ **smolder** _____ *with rage but say nothing.*

SYNONYMS: to simmer, fester, seethe, fume, stew
ANTONYMS: to blaze; to explode

10. trudge
('trəj)

(v.) to walk or march slowly and with difficulty or tiredness
At the end of a long day, workers _____ **trudge** _____ *home.*

(n.) a long, tiring walk
If I miss the bus, it's a two-mile _____ **trudge** _____ *to school.*

SYNONYMS: to plod, slog, tramp; a hike
ANTONYMS: to prance, race, hurry

11. volunteer
(vä lən 'tir)

(n.) a person who chooses to join or to do a service; someone who gives time or effort without pay
_____ **Volunteers** _____ *are needed at the children's hospital.*

(v.) to offer one's services; to do or say freely
Who will _____ **volunteer** _____ *to set the dinner table?*

SYNONYMS: an unpaid person; voluntary; to enlist; to offer
ANTONYMS: an employee, draftee; paid, hired; to force, draft

12. weary
('wir ē)

(adj.) feeling tired, worn out; having no more patience
When I have to do a boring task, I become _____ **weary** _____.

(v.) to make tired; to grow tired
A dull speech may _____ **weary** _____ *an audience.*

SYNONYMS: exhausted, drained, fatigued, drooping, sleepy
ANTONYMS: fresh, lively, energetic; tolerant; to enliven, energize

 **Match the Meaning**

For each item below choose the word whose meaning is suggested by the clue given. Then write the word in the space provided.

1. A measured portion of food is called a _____ration_____.
   a. clatter   b. gallant   c. trudge   d. ration

2. A fire that burns without flame but with smoke _____smolders_____.
   a. volunteers   b. reserves   c. smolders   d. clatters

3. If you have to _____trudge_____ through deep snow, your journey will be difficult.
   a. volunteer   b. trudge   c. ration   d. scholar

4. A(n) _____gallant_____ action is one that is courteous and brave.
   a. gallant   b. awkward   c. lukewarm   d. weary

5. A _____lukewarm_____ shower is neither hot nor cold.
   a. plentiful   b. weary   c. gallant   d. lukewarm

6. When horses' hooves clop on the pavement, they can be said to _____clatter_____.
   a. volunteer   b. clatter   c. reserve   d. trudge

7. A social situation that is embarrassing and hard to handle can be termed _____awkward_____.
   a. awkward   b. lukewarm   c. plentiful   d. weary

8. An expert in the law may be known as a legal _____scholar_____.
   a. gallant   b. reserve   c. scholar   d. volunteer

9. If you have more than enough of something, you have a(n) _____plentiful_____ amount.
   a. awkward   b. plentiful   c. weary   d. lukewarm

10. A long period of hard work is likely to leave a person feeling _____weary_____.
    a. awkward   b. lukewarm   c. plentiful   d. weary

11. A cook may _____reserve_____ leftover food to be eaten at a later date.
    a. clatter   b. volunteer   c. reserve   d. smolder

12. If you _____volunteer_____ your services, you will not be paid.
    a. volunteer   b. ration   c. clatter   d. reserve

Synonyms

*For each item below choose the word that is most nearly the **same** in meaning as the word or phrase in **boldface**. Then write your choice on the line provided.*

1. a well-known academic **authority**
   a. gallant   b. volunteer   c. reserve   d. scholar   _____scholar_____

2. **exhausted** after the race
   a. weary   b. plentiful   c. lukewarm   d. awkward   _____weary_____

3. heard the **racket** of the tire chains
   a. reserve   b. scholar   c. ration   d. clatter   _____clatter_____

4. **plodded** through the mud
   a. smoldered   b. trudged   c. volunteered   d. clattered   _____trudged_____

5. **gave out** the treats
   a. volunteered   b. clattered   c. rationed   d. smoldered   _____rationed_____

6. an **unpaid** teacher's aide
   a. gallant   b. volunteer   c. weary   d. lukewarm   _____volunteer_____

Antonyms

*For each item below choose the word that is most nearly **opposite** in meaning to the word or phrase in **boldface**. Then write your choice on the line provided.*

1. **scarce** resources
   a. lukewarm   b. plentiful   c. awkward   d. volunteer   _____plentiful_____

2. a **graceful** gesture
   a. volunteer   b. gallant   c. weary   d. awkward   _____awkward_____

3. a bowl of **steaming** soup
   a. awkward   b. weary   c. lukewarm   d. plentiful   _____lukewarm_____

4. **wasted** our energy
   a. smoldered   b. volunteered   c. reserved   d. clattered   _____reserved_____

5. watched the logs in the fireplace **blaze**
   a. clatter   b. smolder   c. volunteer   d. trudge   _____smolder_____

6. **cowardly** behavior
   a. gallant   b. volunteer   c. awkward   d. lukewarm   _____gallant_____

Completing the Sentence

From the list of words on pages 60–61, choose the one that best completes each item below. Write the word in the space provided. (You may have to change the word's ending.)

A GROUP EFFORT

■ Everyone in town complained that the park was a mess. Our school decided to do something about it. We _____**volunteered**_____ to clean it up.

■ Last Saturday we got to work. We began by picking up trash. The bottles and cans _____**clattered**_____ when we tossed them into recycling bins.

■ Then we went to work on the plants and the lawns. It was _____**awkward**_____ for the smaller children to use big brooms and rakes, but they did their best.

■ We gathered all the fallen leaves and sticks and broken branches into a big heap to make a bonfire. One of the teachers lit the pile, and we all watched as it _____**smoldered**_____ for a while. Finally it burst into flame.

■ By four o'clock, we were _____**weary**_____ and ready to call it a day.

■ We stood back to admire our work. The park looked beautiful! Everyone cheered. Then we _____**trudged**_____ home proudly. We were ready for cold drinks and hot showers.

AFTER THE FIGHTING ENDED

■ Many _____**scholars**_____ have spent years studying what happened during and after World War II. They have written hundreds of books about what life was like in Europe after the fighting ended.

■ Getting something to eat was difficult. Crops had been destroyed, and many farm animals had been killed or starved to death. _____**Rations**_____ were in short supply.

■ Some families had managed to stash a few items in _____**reserve**_____, but thousands were hungry.

■ Fuel for heat was very scarce. It was a luxury just to have some _____**lukewarm**_____ water for a bath.

■ Kind and _____**gallant**_____ soldiers gave their sweaters and blankets to shivering children and old people.

■ Even though life was hard and people had to struggle to get by, one thing was truly _____**plentiful**_____: hope for the future.

Word Associations

*Circle the letter next to the word or expression that best completes the sentence or answers the question. Pay special attention to the word in **boldface.***

1. Someone who feels **awkward** in front of an audience might
   a. try out for the talent show
   b. become an opera singer
   c. join the debating team
   (d.) avoid the drama club

2. Books are usually **plentiful**
   a. in a zoo
   (b.) in a library
   c. in a hospital
   d. in a laundromat

3. A **smoldering** home was recently
   (a.) on fire
   b. painted
   c. sold
   d. built

4. If milk is **rationed**, expect
   (a.) a small serving of milk
   b. all the juice you want
   c. a glass of water
   d. nothing at all to drink

5. To **reserve** a library book, you
   a. borrow a friend's copy
   b. go to a bookstore
   (c.) put your name on a list
   d. make a photocopy of it

6. You would measure a **trudge**
   a. by the inch
   b. by the foot
   c. by the yard
   (d.) by the mile

7. A **gallant** act on a cold day is
   a. to throw snowballs
   b. to zip up your jacket
   (c.) to offer your gloves to a friend
   d. to stay inside during recess

8. With crowds or traffic **clattering** by, it would be very hard to
   a. cook a healthy supper
   b. find the nearest bus stop
   (c.) have a quiet conversation
   d. climb a stepladder

9. To **volunteer** information, you'd
   a. join the school band
   (b.) freely tell what you know
   c. get paid
   d. hire librarians

10. **Weary** tourists might
    (a.) sit down and rest
    b. get up very early
    c. stay out all night
    d. work out at a gym

11. Which is probably **lukewarm**?
    a. a frosty pitcher of lemonade
    b. an ice-cream cone
    c. a steaming pot of soup
    (d.) a half-empty mug of cocoa

12. A **scholar** probably spent years
    a. sewing
    (b.) studying
    c. eating
    d. dancing

Selecting Word Meanings

*For each of the following items circle the choice that is most nearly the **same** in meaning as the word in **boldface**.*

1. made the plates **clatter**
   a. slip   b. rattle   c. break   d. drop

2. unable to **penetrate** the surface
   a. clean   b. paint   c. cover   d. pierce

3. the **policy** against smoking
   a. guidelines   b. insurance   c. deadline   d. sign

4. had to **ration** the supplies
   a. store   b. purchase   c. distribute   d. waste

5. a period of severe **drought**
   a. heat   b. rain   c. cold   d. dryness

6. a deadly **epidemic**
   a. infection   b. weapon   c. poison   d. accident

7. **lash** the cartons to the truck
   a. examine   b. carry   c. strap   d. unload

8. **smolder** with anger
   a. speak   b. seethe   c. explode   d. act

9. tucked away in my **baggage**
   a. garbage   b. closet   c. wallet   d. suitcases

10. a **lukewarm** response
    a. half-hearted   b. enthusiastic   c. friendly   d. hostile

11. **content** to stay home
    a. disappointed   b. unable   c. satisfied   d. required

12. tried not to **envy** their success
    a. copy   b. long for   c. notice   d. object to

*For each item below study the **boldface** word in which there is a blank. If a letter is missing, fill in the blank to make a correctly spelled word. If the word is already spelled correctly, leave the blank empty.*

1. gave **ac_c_urate** answers

2. a natural **di_s_aster**

3. wish for **etern_a_l** youth

4. **h_u_mid** air

5. **op__pose** the idea

6. a **plent_i_ful** harvest

7. **reserv_e_** the date

8. a respected **sc_h_olar**

9. **sur__vive** the injury

10. **volun_t_eer** for the job

11. a **stap__le** of our diet

12. a famous **an_c_estor**

Antonyms

*For each of the following items circle the choice that is most nearly the **opposite** in meaning to the word in **boldface**.*

1. a **constant** source of energy
   a. continuous   b. instant   c. expensive   (d.) irregular

2. **gallant** warriors
   a. noble   (b.) cowardly   c. enemy   d. weary

3. required **haste**
   (a.) slowness   b. time   c. money   d. speed

4. a **pioneer** in science
   a. trailblazer   b. expert   (c.) follower   d. student

5. **awkward** on the dance floor
   a. unskilled   b. comic   (c.) graceful   d. clumsy

6. an **elementary** course
   a. enjoyable   (b.) advanced   c. interesting   d. difficult

7. **establish** a reputation
   a. question   b. earn   c. build   (d.) ruin

8. seemed to **blossom** overight
   (a.) wither   b. disappear   c. flower   d. change

Vocabulary in Context

Words have been left out of the following passage. For each numbered item in the passage, fill in the circle next to the word in the margin that best fills the blank space. Then answer each question below by writing a sentence that contains one of the words you have chosen.

People who drive in __1__ weather should be very careful. Snow, sleet, heavy rain, and ice make roads slippery. High winds and fog can make it hard to see. If drivers have to make sudden stops, their cars can spin out of control.

Road conditions affect how cars move and stop. In bad weather cars may __2__. Some small accidents are known as "fender benders." In a fender bender the people in the cars usually do not get hurt because the cars are not traveling very fast. Most of the time the cars can be driven away without having to be towed, and the damage is __3__. Fender benders are more scary than deadly.

Unfortunately, accidents may happen even in perfect weather. They may occur if drivers take their minds off their driving even for a moment. Experienced drivers always pay attention to what they are doing. They know how important it is to stay __4__ to other cars around them, to traffic signals, and to people and animals that may be crossing the road. That is why driver's education classes put so much emphasis on caution and safety.

1. ○ sensible
   ○ feeble
   ○ humid
   ● foul

2. ○ volunteer
   ● collide
   ○ clatter
   ○ romp

3. ● slight
   ○ plentiful
   ○ lukewarm
   ○ elementary

4. ○ tidy
   ○ weary
   ● alert
   ○ content

5. What might happen if drivers do not pay attention?

   If drivers are not **alert**, they can get into accidents.

6. How would you rate the damage that occurs in a fender bender?

   It is usually **slight**.

7. What kind of weather can be a problem for drivers?

   Drivers must be very careful in **foul** weather.

8. What may happen to cars in bad weather?

   They may spin out of control or **collide**.

Analogies *In each of the following circle the letter for the item that best completes the comparison. Then explain the relationship on the lines provided.*

1. sensible is to **foolish** as
   a. eternal is to everlasting
   b. tidy is to messy
   c. accurate is to exact
   d. constant is to continuous

Relationship: "Sensible" and "foolish" are antonyms/opposite in meaning; "tidy" and "messy" are antonyms/opposite in meaning.

2. feeble is to **weak** as
   a. staple is to unnecessary
   b. worthy is to useless
   c. epidemic is to limited
   d. antique is to ancient

Relationship: "Feeble" and "weak" are synonyms/mean the same; "antique" and "ancient" are synonyms/mean the same.

3. trudge is to **hurry** as
   a. smolder is to blaze
   b. digest is to absorb
   c. distract is to sidetrack
   d. blossom is to flourish

Relationship: "Trudge" and "hurry" are antonyms/opposite in meaning; "smolder" and "blaze" are antonyms/opposite in meaning.

4. quiver is to **archer** as
   a. dugout is to pitcher
   b marathon is to runner
   c. backpack is to hiker
   d. medal is to skater

Relationship: A quiver is used/carried by an archer; a backpack is used/carried by a hiker.

Challenge: Make up your own
Write a comparison using the words in the box below. (Hint: There are three possible analogies.) Then write the relationship on the lines provided.

petal	page	grief	scholar
pioneer	disaster	triumph	flower
joy	study	book	explore

Analogy: _____ is to _____ as _____ is to _____ .

Relationship: See Table of Contents

Word Families

*The words in **boldface** in the sentences below are related to words introduced in Units 5–8. For example, the adjectives* worthless *and* hasty *in item 1 are related to the adjective* worthy *and the noun* haste *(both in Unit 5). Based on your under standing of the unit words, circle the related word in **boldface** that best completes each sentence.*

scholar	humid	distract	envy	noble
content	establish	weary	volunteer	survive
accurate	worthy	antique	penetrate	oppose
reserve	collide	haste	ancestor	disaster

1. Now that the movie theater has closed, the free passes that we won are (**worthless**/**hasty**).

2. Many people are interested in tracing their (**scholarship**/**ancestry**) back hundreds of years.

3. There was strong (**opposition**/**establishment**) when the governor announced new taxes.

4. Scientists predicted the (**collision**/**weariness**) between a comet and a moon of Jupiter.

5. In the wild, (**accuracy**/**survival**) depends on an animal's ability to find food, water, and safety.

6. A(n) (**envious**/**disastrous**) fire burned for days and ruined thousands of acres of forest.

7. Tropical plants and flowers grow best in high (**nobility**/**humidity**).

8. Adding machines are (**antiquated**/**voluntary**) compared with today's small, quiet, high-speed calculators.

9. We made a (**penetration**/**reservation**) for dinner next week at our favorite restaurant.

10. The street noise was such a (**distraction**/**contentment**) that it was hard to have a simple conversation.

Word Games

Something is missing! Find and ring the words from Units 5–8 that are hidden in the grid below. Then choose from these words the ones that best complete the sentences that follow. Write the words in the blanks.

D	I	G	E	S	T	X	F	P	R
R	H	L	P	R	D	Z	N	O	D
O	M	O	N	F	E	E	B	L	E
U	Y	D	U	H	M	C	Z	I	N
G	R	I	F	O	U	L	R	C	W
H	L	W	R	P	A	A	L	Y	Z
T	I	D	Y	P	M	T	P	Q	A
Z	E	A	V	O	G	T	T	D	Q
W	A	Q	K	S	H	E	U	Z	L
D	C	L	M	E	P	R	O	M	P

1. "This looks like a case of _____ **foul** _____ play," said the detective.

2. "Shush!" said the librarian. "Stop that _____ **clatter** _____."

3. "Take the puppies outside to _____ **romp** _____ and play," said Dad.

4. "Today's rain will bring relief from the long, hot _____ **drought** _____," said the weather forecaster.

5. "If you chew your food well, it will be easy to _____ **digest** _____," said Mom.

6. "It is our _____ **policy** _____ to give a full refund if the item you buy does not work," said the store manager.

Definitions

Choose the word from the box that matches each definition. Write the word on the line provided. The first one has been done for you.

haul	clatter	disaster	constant	~~counsel~~
digest	competition	envy	ambush	humid
indicate	previous	obtain	penetrate	noble
stun	suitable	vanity	weary	yield

1. a lawyer in a legal case   <u>counsel</u>

2. trying to outdo others; a game or contest   <u>competition</u>

3. the product or amount made or produced   <u>yield</u>

4. to understand or grasp an idea   <u>digest</u>

5. loyal, steady, or faithful   <u>constant</u>

6. to want what others have   <u>envy</u>

7. to move by pulling, dragging, or carting   <u>haul</u>

8. coming before in time or order   <u>previous</u>

9. to shock, daze; to make unable to feel, react, or think   <u>stun</u>

10. to pass through, enter, grasp, soak, or see into   <u>penetrate</u>

11. a hard, rattling sound; noisy chattering   <u>clatter</u>

12. the quality of being stuck-up or vain   <u>vanity</u>

13. feeling tired, worn out; having no more patience   <u>weary</u>

14. steamy or heavy with moisture; damp   <u>humid</u>

15. to gain or get through some effort   <u>obtain</u>

Antonyms

*Choose the word from the box that is most nearly **opposite** in meaning to each group of words. Write the word on the line provided. The first one has been done for you.*

1. an unknown, a nobody _____celebrity_____
2. to expand, enlarge _____contract_____
3. offensive, unappealing _____attractive_____
4. courage, excitement _____dread_____
5. modern, new, current, fresh _____antique_____
6. to shrink, wither, fade _____blossom_____
7. unimportant, minor, unnecessary _____essential_____
8. to refuse, deny, disallow _____consent_____
9. fair, honest, clean, pure _____foul_____
10. secondary, complex, advanced _____elementary_____
11. to splurge, squander, waste _____reserve_____
12. a draftee _____volunteer_____
13. useless, no-good _____worthy_____
14. random, irregular, unusual _____routine_____
15. to empower, raise up _____humble_____
16. calm, careful, orderly _____frantic_____
17. mistaken, false, misleading _____accurate_____
18. flattery, praise, a compliment _____slight_____
19. gentle, tender, kindly _____stern_____
20. fleeting, short, temporary, brief _____eternal_____

accurate
antique
attractive
blossom
~~celebrity~~
consent
contract
demonstrate
dread
elementary
essential
eternal
foul
frantic
gallant
humble
pioneer
reserve
routine
slight
sponsor
stern
sturdy
volunteer
worthy

Completing the Sentence

Choose the word from the box that best completes each sentence below. Write the word in the space provided. The first one has been done for you.

Group A

contribute	thaw	hardship	employ
sincere	urgent	neglect	shabby

1. We decided to _____**contribute**_____ thirty dollars to the fund for new gym equipment.

2. It is never a _____**hardship**_____ to take care of my friend's playful puppy.

3. If you _____**neglect**_____ your teeth, you may get cavities, develop sore gums, or even lose a tooth.

4. When we moved to our new house, we replaced our _____**shabby**_____ old dining room table.

5. After Monday's cold snap, it took several days for the stream behind our school to _____**thaw**_____.

Group B

alert	collide	feeble	haste
oppose	policy	noble	trudge

1. Some people who _____**oppose**_____ cruel treatment of animals decide to become vegetarians.

2. Many American students memorize the _____**noble**_____ words of the Declaration of Independence.

3. People in a hurry often eat with such _____**haste**_____ that they end up getting heartburn.

4. Parents should always give a baby-sitter the phone numbers of people to _____**alert**_____ in case of emergency.

5. My dad's company has a _____**policy**_____ that permits employees to wear casual clothing on Fridays.

Classifying

Choose the word from the box that goes best with each group of words. Write the word in the space provided. Then explain what the words have in common. The first one has been done for you.

annual	baggage	basic	~~calculate~~	dependable
drought	drowsy	lukewarm	quiver	romp

1. estimate, compute, _____**calculate**_____

   The words name mathematical operations.

2. sleepy, sluggish, _____**drowsy**_____

   The words are synonyms.

3. bow, arrow, _____**quiver**_____

   The words name objects used in archery.

4. hot, _____**lukewarm**_____, cold

   The words describe temperatures.

5. daily, weekly, monthly, _____**annual**_____

   The words describe periods of time.

6. _____**basic**_____, intermediate, advanced

   The words describe levels of difficulty.

7. reliable, responsible, _____**dependable**_____

   The words are synonyms.

8. suitcases, trunks, _____**baggage**_____

   The words name objects used by travelers.

9. famine, epidemic, plague, _____**drought**_____

   The words describe natural disasters.

10. stomp, clomp, _____**romp**_____

    The words describe ways of moving. The words rhyme.

UNIT 9

Definitions

Study the spelling, pronunciation, part of speech, and definition given for each of the words below. Write the word in the blank space in the sentence that follows. Then read the synonyms and antonyms.

1. **convict**
   (*v.*, kən ′vikt;
   n., ′kän vikt)

   (v.) to prove or judge to be guilty
   The jury voted to _____ **convict** _____ *the defendant.*
   (n.) a person who has been proved guilty of a crime and sentenced to prison; someone who is serving a long prison term
   In a prison a _____ **convict** _____ *is usually given a job to do.*
   SYNONYMS: to condemn, sentence; a prisoner, inmate, felon, criminal
   ANTONYMS: to acquit, free, release

2. **discipline**
   (′di sə plən)

   (n.) punishment; training that results in obedience and self-control; orderly behavior; control gained by enforcing rules of conduct; a branch of knowledge
   Drill instructors insist on strict military _____ **discipline** _____.
   (v.) to punish; to train in proper behavior; to bring under control
   The principal knows how to _____ **discipline** _____ *rowdy students.*
   SYNONYMS: correction, control, direction, drill, practice; to correct, chastise, penalize, subdue, limit
   ANTONYMS: confusion, disorder, rebellion; to forgive

3. **dungeon**
   (′dən jən)

   (n.) a dark room or cell used as a prison, usually underground
   The story described the terror of being locked in a _____ **dungeon** _____.
   SYNONYMS: a keep, hold, hole

4. **earnest**
   (′ər nəst)

   (adj.) serious, important, or grave
   An _____ **earnest** _____ *desire to help others may lead a person to choose a career in medicine.*
   SYNONYMS: intent, solemn
   ANTONYMS: insincere, trivial, frivolous, foolish

5. **enclose**
   (in ′klōz)

   (v.) to surround on every side; to close up in or fence off; to include with something else
   Be sure to _____ **enclose** _____ *payment with the bill.*
   SYNONYMS: to confine, cage; to cover, encircle, envelop; to include, insert
   ANTONYMS: to release, free; to omit, exclude, leave out

6. **gradual**
   (′gra jə wəl)

   (adj.) happening step-by-step or by degrees; changing little by little
   There may be _____ **gradual** _____ *improvement in a patient's condition after surgery.*
   SYNONYMS: moderate, slow, steady
   ANTONYMS: sudden, abrupt

When they are hatched and for the first few months of their lives, birds must rely upon their parents to **nourish** (word 9) them.

7. **grumble**
('grəm bəl)

(v.) to complain angrily but not loudly; to growl
Many people _____grumble_____ when they have to wait on a long line.

(n.) a growling sound; a muttered complaint
The announcement of the delay brought a _____grumble_____ from the passengers.

SYNONYMS: to mutter, rumble, mumble; to complain, fuss; a protest

8. **jagged**
('ja gəd)

(adj.) with a rough or sharp edge; irregular or harsh
I cut my hand on a _____jagged_____ piece of broken glass.

SYNONYMS: ragged, serrated; uneven, rugged
ANTONYMS: smooth, even, regular

9. **nourish**
('nər ish)

(v.) to feed or help grow and develop; to support
A teacher works to _____nourish_____ a love of learning in students.

SYNONYMS: to nurture, raise, provide for, cherish; to foster, maintain, sustain
ANTONYMS: to starve, neglect, abandon

10. **provision**
(prə 'vi zhən)

(n.) the act of supplying or making available; a stock of food or supplies; a step taken ahead of time; a condition, as in a contract
A good hotel makes every possible _____provision_____ for the comfort of its guests.

(v.) to supply with food or materials
It takes tons of food to _____provision_____ an army.

SYNONYMS: an arrangement, preparation; a requirement; to furnish, stock

11. **treaty**
('trē tē)

(n.) an agreement or contract between two or more countries, arrived at by discussion and compromise; the legal document that has the terms of such an agreement
The warring nations finally signed a peace _____treaty_____.

SYNONYMS: a pact, settlement, accord

12. **uneasy**
(ən 'ē zē)

(adj.) feeling worried or unsure; causing discomfort
I often feel _____uneasy_____ before a final exam.

SYNONYMS: troubled, edgy, disturbed, anxious; jittery, nervous, jumpy
ANTONYMS: relaxed, certain, calm, comfortable

77

Match the Meaning

For each item below choose the word whose meaning is suggested by the clue given. Then write the word in the space provided.

1. Good _____ **discipline** _____ teaches a person self-control.
   a. provision   b. dungeon   c. treaty   d. discipline

2. The cage that _____ **encloses** _____ my parakeet is filled with toys.
   a. nourishes   b. encloses   c. disciplines   d. convicts

3. A written agreement between countries is called a _____ **treaty** _____.
   a. dungeon   b. discipline   c. treaty   d. convict

4. Someone serious in manner might be described as _____ **earnest** _____.
   a. jagged   b. gradual   c. uneasy   d. earnest

5. People who feel awkward or nervous may say they are _____ **uneasy** _____.
   a. uneasy   b. gradual   c. earnest   d. jagged

6. A jury will _____ **convict** _____ a defendant they believe to be guilty.
   a. nourish   b. convict   c. provision   d. grumble

7. Human hair and fingernails grow at a(n) _____ **gradual** _____ rate.
   a. gradual   b. earnest   c. jagged   d. uneasy

8. The castle had a dark _____ **dungeon** _____ for captives.
   a. convict   b. provision   c. dungeon   d. treaty

9. If you drop a glass, it will probably break into _____ **jagged** _____ pieces.
   a. gradual   b. jagged   c. uneasy   d. earnest

10. To complain in a low but angry voice is to _____ **grumble** _____.
    a. grumble   b. convict   c. enclose   d. nourish

11. Before you go away on vacation, you should make _____ **provisions** _____ for someone to take care of your pet.
    a. convicts   b. disciplines   c. provisions   d. dungeons

12. Adults help babies to grow and develop by _____ **nourishing** _____ them.
    a. nourishing   b. enclosing   c. disciplining   d. grumbling

78 ■ Unit 9

Synonyms

*For each item below choose the word that is most nearly the **same** in meaning as the word or phrase in **boldface**. Then write your choice on the line provided.*

1. a **solemn** apology
   a. gradual   b. jagged   c. uneasy   d. earnest   _____ earnest _____

2. alone in the damp **keep**
   a. treaty   b. discipline   c. dungeon   d. provision   _____ dungeon _____

3. signed the **pact** for increased trade
   a. treaty   b. convict   c. dungeon   d. grumble   _____ treaty _____

4. **complain** about the weather
   a. grumble   b. convict   c. enclose   d. nourish   _____ grumble _____

5. **confined** the dogs in the yard
   a. disciplined   b. enclosed   c. nourished   d. convicted   _____ enclosed _____

6. a **condition** of the contract
   a. treaty   b. dungeon   c. provision   d. convict   _____ provision _____

Antonyms

*For each item below choose the word that is most nearly **opposite** in meaning to the word or phrase in **boldface**. Then write your choice on the line provided.*

1. the **even** peaks of the mountain range
   a. gradual   b. jagged   c. uneasy   d. earnest   _____ jagged _____

2. came to a **sudden** stop
   a. uneasy   b. earnest   c. jagged   d. gradual   _____ gradual _____

3. **neglected** the growing plants
   a. nourished   b. disciplined   c. provisioned   d. enclosed   _____ nourished _____

4. **freed** the defendant
   a. disciplined   b. nourished   c. convicted   d. provisioned   _____ convicted _____

5. gave us a **relaxed** smile
   a. uneasy   b. earnest   c. gradual   d. jagged   _____ uneasy _____

6. **disorder** in the classroom
   a. treaties   b. discipline   c. convicts   d. grumbles   _____ discipline _____

Completing the Sentence

From the list of words on pages 76–77, choose the one that best completes each item below. Then write the word in the space provided. (You may have to change the word's ending.)

A FITTING NICKNAME

■ A frontier town was a rough and often lawless place. There was such a lack of order and _____ **discipline** _____ that the frontier became know as the "Wild West."

■ Today when people are accused of committing crimes, they get their day in court. But frontier towns did not always bother with a judge and jury. Angry mobs or enemies out for revenge often _____ **convicted** _____ people on the spot.

■ In an attempt to bring some order to life, many towns enacted _____ **provisions** _____ that required people to leave their weapons with the sheriff when they came to town.

■ There were complaints, but the system led to a(n) _____ **uneasy** _____ peace. People still could not feel sure that they were safe.

■ Law and order did not come overnight; but settlers did see a(n) _____ **gradual** _____ improvement in law enforcement.

TEARS WITHOUT TEARS

■ If you accidentally tear a dollar bill in half, your first reaction may be to _____ **grumble** _____ or cry. But all is not lost!

■ Don't bother trying to tape, paste, or staple the _____ **jagged** _____ edges of the bill back together.

■ Just _____ **enclose** _____ the pieces in an envelope and take them to a bank. A teller will give you a new bill in exchange for the torn one.

FAIR CARE

■ International _____ **treaties** _____ state that prisoners of war must receive decent and humane treatment at the hands of their captors.

■ Whether they are held in damp _____ **dungeons** _____ or modern jails, prisoners must be given food, water, and basic medical care.

■ Some may be allowed to read or write to _____ **nourish** _____ their minds and spirits.

■ Unfortunately, some nations have not made a(n) _____ **earnest** _____ effort to treat prisoners decently. A number of human rights groups work hard to force these nations to take these rules seriously.

*Circle the letter next to the word or expression that best completes the sentence or answers the question. Pay special attention to the word in **boldface**.*

1. A teacher who demands strict **discipline** might say
   a. "Shall we start math now?"
   b. "Let's skip spelling today."
   c. "Raise your hand to talk."
   d. "Chat all you want today."

2. Which of these is **jagged**?
   a. a bowl of spaghetti
   b. a baseball cap
   c. a ball of yarn
   d. a saw blade

3. It's likely a **dungeon** would be
   a. warm and fuzzy
   b. hot and humid
   c. cozy and homey
   d. dark and damp

4. You know I feel **uneasy** because
   a. I smile all the time
   b. I stand up straight
   c. my clothes are new
   d. my hands are shaking

5. **Earnest** students would
   a. pay attention in class
   b. not care about school
   c. walk to school
   d. sleep in class

6. Which would **nourish** a kitten?
   a. a big dog
   b. a bowl of milk
   c. a catnip toy
   d. a flea collar

7. Which best **encloses** a yard?
   a. a stream
   b. a highway
   c. a fence
   d. a cage

8. Lunch **provisions** may include
   a. hungry people
   b. posters about good health
   c. bread for sandwiches
   d. tubes of toothpaste

9. If **convicts** get away, they escape
   a. from the scene of a crime
   b. from kitchen chores
   c. from jail
   d. from the circus

10. When I **grumble**, I
    a. do my homework
    b. complain a lot
    c. raise my voice
    d. go to the movies

11. Two nations sign a **treaty** if
    a. they both agree
    b. they both want a party
    c. they both raise taxes
    d. both go to war

12. During a **gradual** warming spell, temperatures may go
    a. from 65° F to 25° F
    b. from 65° F to 67° F
    c. from 65° F to 99° F
    d. from 65° F to 55° F

UNIT 10

Definitions

Study the spelling, pronunciation, part of speech, and definition given for each of the words below. Write the word in the blank space in the sentence that follows. Then read the synonyms and antonyms.

1. **distress**
   (di 'stres)

   (n.) deep worry or suffering; being in danger or in trouble
   The Coast Guard helps boats in _____distress_____ .

   (v.) to trouble or upset; to cause worry or stress; to make unhappy
   Our dogs, who bark at every noise, may _____distress_____ *our sick neighbor.*

   SYNONYMS: anguish, anxiety, grief, torment; to upset, bother, disturb, irritate
   ANTONYMS: calm, joy, delight; to calm, gladden, comfort, soothe

2. **drench**
   (drench)

   (v.) to wet or soak through and through; to cover or fill completely
   A night of rain is enough to _____drench_____ *the field.*

   SYNONYMS: to saturate, flood, douse, sop, drown
   ANTONYMS: to dry, parch

3. **dwell**
   (dwel)

   (v.) to live, especially in a particular place; to remain, stay; to keep one's attention on something
   Do you think that human beings will one day _____dwell_____ *on the moon?*

   SYNONYMS: to inhabit, reside; to linger, last

4. **juvenile**
   ('jü və nīl)

   (adj.) not fully grown; of or meant for children or young people; foolish or immature
   His _____juvenile_____ *pranks are so annoying!*

   (n.) a young person or individual
   The play has a big part for a _____juvenile_____ .

   SYNONYMS: young, youthful, childish; a youth, minor
   ANTONYMS: mature, developed; an adult

5. **outstanding**
   (aút 'stan diŋ)

   (adj.) standing apart from others due to being excellent; unpaid
   The firefighter was praised for her _____outstanding_____ *bravery.*

   SYNONYMS: remarkable, great, noteworthy, unusual, superior; unpaid
   ANTONYMS: ordinary, regular, usual, average

6. **proceed**
   (prō 'sēd)

   (v.) to go on or continue in an orderly way; to start again after a pause; to start an action, move
   We must _____proceed_____ *directly to a hospital.*

   SYNONYMS: to advance, progress
   ANTONYMS: to recede, retreat, stand, stay, stop

82

Helicopters can help people in **distress** (word 1) in areas that are difficult or impossible to reach with rescue vehicles.

7. **register**
('re je stər)

(n.) an official record book; the range of a voice or musical instrument; a machine that records data

How many names are on the class _____register_____ *?*

(v.) to sign up; to show on a scale; to note or understand

When must we _____register_____ *for Little League?*

SYNONYMS: a roster, catalog, ledger; to enroll, enlist, join; to express, demonstrate
ANTONYMS: to withdraw

8. **sift**
(sift)

(v.) to put through a strainer to separate or break up lumps; to sort through or examine

It took some time to _____sift_____ *through all the mail.*

SYNONYMS: to separate, strain, filter, screen; to examine, study

9. **spree**
(sprē)

(n.) a lively or wild outburst of activity

The prize was a thirty-minute shopping _____spree_____ *.*

SYNONYMS: a riot, binge, bash, fling, splurge

10. **tardy**
('tär dē)

(adj.) not on time, delayed; slow-moving

Have you ever been _____tardy_____ *for school?*

SYNONYMS: late, overdue; sluggish
ANTONYMS: early, prompt

11. **unfit**
(ən 'fit)

(adj.) not suitable or proper; not good enough; unhealthy

The flood made tap water _____unfit_____ *to drink.*

SYNONYMS: bad, improper, inappropriate, inadequate, unqualified; incompetent
ANTONYMS: suitable, proper, appropriate, qualified; healthy, fit, sound

12. **variety**
(və 'rī tē)

(n.) change, lack of sameness; a number of different forms or types; a category of plants or animals

The old saying has it that " _____variety_____ *is the spice of life."*

SYNONYMS: diversity, difference; an assortment, selection
ANTONYMS: sameness, unity

Match the Meaning

For each item below choose the word whose meaning is suggested by the clue given. Then write the word in the space provided.

1. In most stores you will find a cash _____**register**_____ .
   a. distress   b. spree   c. variety   d. register

2. To soak something with water is to _____**drench**_____ it.
   a. proceed   b. drench   c. register   d. sift

3. Eat a _____**variety**_____ of foods to avoid boring meals.
   a. spree   b. register   c. variety   d. distress

4. An _____**outstanding**_____ book is one that is much better than most.
   a. unfit   b. tardy   c. juvenile   d. outstanding

5. To live in a particular place is to _____**dwell**_____ there.
   a. dwell   b. drench   c. sift   d. distress

6. One who suffers great pain is in _____**distress**_____ .
   a. register   b. distress   c. juvenile   d. variety

7. If I'm not on time, I'm _____**tardy**_____ .
   a. tardy   b. outstanding   c. unfit   d. juvenile

8. A lively outburst of activity is a _____**spree**_____ .
   a. distress   b. register   c. spree   d. variety

9. Spoiled food is _____**unfit**_____ to eat.
   a. tardy   b. unfit   c. juvenile   d. outstanding

10. People _____**sift**_____ soil to break apart lumps.
    a. sift   b. distress   c. drench   d. register

11. A book meant for young people might be described as _____**juvenile**_____ .
    a. outstanding   b. unfit   c. juvenile   d. tardy

12. Football games _____**proceed**_____ in almost any weather.
    a. proceed   b. drench   c. register   d. distress

Synonyms

For each item below choose the word that is most nearly the **same** in meaning as the word or phrase in **boldface**. Then write your choice on the line provided.

1. a memory that **lingers**
   a. registers   b. dwells   c. distresses   d. drenches   __dwells__

2. a berry-eating **binge**
   a. distress   b. variety   c. juvenile   d. spree   __spree__

3. the wide **assortment** of colors
   a. variety   b. distress   c. spree   d. register   __variety__

4. **scatter** cinnamon into the batter
   a. sift   b. distress   c. drench   d. proceed   __sift__

5. to **saturate** the paper
   a. register   b. drench   c. proceed   d. sift   __drench__

6. the latest **roster** of players
   a. spree   b. distress   c. register   d. juvenile   __register__

Antonyms

For each item below choose the word that is most nearly **opposite** in meaning to the word or phrase in **boldface**. Then write your choice on the line provided.

1. **qualified** to run a marathon
   a. tardy   b. unfit   c. juvenile   d. outstanding   __unfit__

2. is known for being **prompt**
   a. juvenile   b. tardy   c. unfit   d. outstanding   __tardy__

3. **average** strength
   a. juvenile   b. tardy   c. outstanding   d. unfit   __outstanding__

4. **mature** sense of humor
   a. unfit   b. outstanding   c. juvenile   d. tardy   __juvenile__

5. decided to **retreat**
   a. proceed   b. register   c. sift   d. drench   __proceed__

6. to **comfort** the children
   a. distress   b. proceed   c. register   d. drench   __distress__

Completing the Sentence

From the list of words on pages 82–83, choose the one that best completes each item below. Then write the word in the space provided. (You may have to change the word's ending.)

AN APPLE A DAY

■ There are many _____**varieties**_____ of apples available today. You can usually find four or five kinds in the local supermarket.

■ The McIntosh is a(n) _____**outstanding**_____ apple to eat raw—one of the finest—but it turns to mush when you cook it.

■ Bruised apples may be _____**unfit**_____ to serve fresh, but they are perfectly suitable for making tasty applesauce.

HOW TO LOSE A RACE

■ We were supposed to _____**register**_____ by noon on Saturday for the big bicycle race.

■ We planned to enter the _____**juvenile**_____ division, which was for kids under thirteen.

■ But we got involved in a Saturday morning cartoon _____**spree**_____, and we lost track of time.

■ That's often what happens when you _____**dwell**_____ in front of a television.

■ When we got to the park at 12:30 P.M., we found that we were too _____**tardy**_____ to sign up. We had only ourselves to blame for being so late.

LIBRARY EMERGENCY

■ Yesterday the fire station got a _____**distress**_____ call from the public library. There was some kind of trouble there.

■ A crew _____**proceeded**_____ quickly to the building, expecting to see flames and smoke.

■ Instead they found hundreds of books _____**drenched**_____ with water from a broken pipe.

■ Worried librarians _____**sifted**_____ through the mess to find any books they could save. Fortunately some of the books on the bottom shelves were still dry.

*Circle the letter next to the word or expression that best completes the sentence or answers the question. Pay special attention to the word in **boldface**.*

1. In a **register** you might find
   a. shoes
   b. records
   c. gloves
   d. sandwiches

2. Milk is **unfit** to drink if it is
   a. cold
   b. expensive
   c. sour
   d. flavored

3. If I'm **tardy**, I might be told
   a. "You're early!"
   b. "You're lost!"
   c. "Thank you."
   d. "You're late!"

4. Which is a **juvenile**?
   a. a grandmother
   b. a newly hatched chick
   c. a police officer
   d. a car seat

5. You might come back from a **spree**
   a. with a lot of packages
   b. with chicken pox
   c. with a haircut
   d. with a snack

6. Which might you **sift**?
   a. flour
   b. relatives
   c. homework
   d. movies

7. At a camp that offers a **variety** of sports, you might
   a. swim, wrestle, and skate
   b. only play volleyball
   c. meet a famous gymnast
   d. get the same food every day

8. Where do bears **dwell**?
   a. in the ocean
   b. in the sky
   c. in a forest
   d. in apartments

9. If you have **outstanding** bills,
   a. you are remarkable
   b. you owe money
   c. you never sit
   d. you dislike being inside

10. If the action **proceeds**,
    a. it stops
    b. it makes you laugh
    c. it makes you cry
    d. it goes on

11. You're **drenched** in jewelry if you
    a. are extremely thirsty
    b. wear many bracelets and rings
    c. are a swimmer
    d. wear dark sunglasses

12. For a friend in **distress**, you'd
    a. probably jump for joy
    b. probably offer help
    c. probably order lunch
    d. probably change your clothes

Definitions

Study the spelling, pronunciation, part of speech, and definition given for each of the words below. Write the word in the blank space in the sentence that follows. Then read the synonyms and antonyms.

1. **blockade**
   (blä 'kād)

   (v.) to close off or keep people or supplies from going in or out
   *Warships may be used to _____ **blockade** _____ a harbor.*

   (n.) the closing off of an enemy nation, city, port, or area, usually by the military; something that closes off or keeps out
   *During the Civil War, the Union forces used a land and sea _____ **blockade** _____ to cut off the city of Charleston, South Carolina.*

   SYNONYMS: to besiege, isolate, obstruct; a siege; a barrier
   ANTONYMS: to open; an opening

2. **chant**
   (chant)

   (v.) to sing; to recite in a tone that varies only a little or not at all
   *Let us _____ **chant** _____ the ancient poems together.*

   (n.) a song in such a tone; words or phrases repeated in rhythm
   *At a soccer match the _____ **chant** _____ of thousands of fans excites the teams to do their best.*

   SYNONYMS: to intone, vocalize; a hymn, incantation, singsong, recitation

3. **despair**
   (di 'spâr)

   (v.) to give up all hope, lose heart
   *We _____ **despair** _____ of ever seeing them again.*

   (n.) total loss of hope; a cause of loss of hope
   *If fear changes to _____ **despair** _____, a person might give up trying.*

   SYNONYMS: hopelessness, dismay, discouragement
   ANTONYMS: to hope, encourage, take heart; hopefulness, cheer, confidence

4. **elevate**
   ('e lə vāt)

   (v.) to raise or lift up; to increase in position or rank; to cheer up; to improve culturally, intellectually, or morally
   *If your foot is swollen, your doctor may tell you to _____ **elevate** _____ it.*

   SYNONYMS: to boost, heighten, hoist; to advance, promote, upgrade
   ANTONYMS: to lower, drop, lessen; to disgrace, demote

5. **extraordinary**
   (ik 'strôr dən er ē)

   (adj.) beyond the usual or expected; highly unusual or rare
   *My best friend has an _____ **extraordinary** _____ singing voice.*

   SYNONYMS: great, exceptional, amazing, remarkable
   ANTONYMS: ordinary, usual, average, run-of-the-mill

6. **heroic**
   (hi 'rō ik)

   (adj.) brave, noble, or larger than life; involving extreme effort
   *Many poems have been written about the _____ **heroic** _____ deeds of ancient warriors.*

   SYNONYMS: courageous, bold, fearless, gallant
   ANTONYMS: cowardly; minimal, trivial

Children often use **chants** (word 2) to help them keep time when they jump rope.

7. **lance**
(lans)

(n.) a long, metal-tipped weapon used by knights or soldiers on horseback; any sharp, pointed instrument that resembles such a weapon
In the Middle Ages, each knight carried a _____lance_____ into battle.
(v.) to pierce with or as if with a lance; to open a wound
A doctor may decide to _____lance_____ an infected blister.
SYNONYMS: a spear, shaft; to puncture, cut, cut open

8. **missionary**
('mi shə ner ē)

(n.) a person on an assignment, often of a religious nature; someone sent by a church to a foreign land to teach religion and do charity work
The life of a _____missionary_____ requires courage and dedication.
(adj.) related to or involved with such an assignment
The peacekeepers worked with a _____missionary_____ spirit.
SYNONYM: a preacher

9. **pointless**
('point ləs)

(adj.) having no meaning or effect
Sometimes it is _____pointless_____ to continue a conversation.
SYNONYMS: senseless, aimless, futile, meaningless, worthless, ineffective, unproductive
ANTONYMS: fitting, meaningful, sensible, effective, valuable

10. **reflect**
(ri 'flekt)

(v.) to throw back, as heat, light, or sound; to give back an image of, as a mirror; to make apparent, show, or demonstrate; to think deeply about
The surface of the lake will _____reflect_____ the clouds in the sky.
SYNONYMS: to mirror, copy, echo, return; to reveal; to consider, ponder, muse
ANTONYMS: to absorb, retain; to disregard, ignore

11. **site**
(sīt)

(n.) a location, scene, or place where something was, is, or will be
Yorktown was the _____site_____ of a famous battle.
SYNONYMS: a spot, location, position

12. **toxic**
('täk sik)

(adj.) poisonous or deadly
A gas mask can filter out _____toxic_____ fumes.
SYNONYMS: dangerous, harmful, venomous, lethal
ANTONYMS: nontoxic, safe, harmless

Match the Meaning

For each item below choose the word whose meaning is suggested by the clue given. Then write the word in the space provided.

1. A cartoon superhero usually has _____**extraordinary**_____ powers.
   a. pointless   b. toxic   c. missionary   d. extraordinary

2. In wartime a country may use a _____**blockade**_____ to keep supplies from reaching the enemy.
   a. missionary   b. chant   c. lance   d. blockade

3. To increase a person's rank or position is to _____**elevate**_____ that person.
   a. reflect   b. elevate   c. blockade   d. chant

4. A _____**lance**_____ is a long spear with a metal point.
   a. site   b. blockade   c. lance   d. missionary

5. If you lose heart when things go badly, you _____**despair**_____.
   a. reflect   b. chant   c. despair   d. lance

6. A brave person whose actions seem larger than life is a _____**heroic**_____ individual.
   a. heroic   b. missionary   c. pointless   d. toxic

7. Mother Theresa was a famous _____**missionary**_____ who helped the poor.
   a. blockade   b. missionary   c. chant   d. site

8. The place where a home is built is called its _____**site**_____.
   a. despair   b. chant   c. site   d. missionary

9. A(n) _____**pointless**_____ remark is one that has no meaning.
   a. heroic   b. pointless   c. missionary   d. extraordinary

10. A song or hymn that is mostly in the same tone is called a _____**chant**_____.
    a. blockade   b. site   c. lance   d. chant

11. Something that is poisonous may be described as _____**toxic**_____.
    a. missionary   b. pointless   c. toxic   d. heroic

12. When a surface gives back an image, it is said to _____**reflect**_____ that image.
    a. reflect   b. elevate   c. blockade   d. despair

Synonyms

*For each item below choose the word that is most nearly the **same** in meaning as the word or phrase in **boldface**. Then write your choice on the line provided.*

1. discovered some **exceptional** fossils
   a. toxic   b. pointless   c. extraordinary d. missionary _____extraordinary_____

2. found the best **spot** for our picnic
   a. chant   b. missionary   c. lance   d. site   _____site_____

3. after the doctor **punctures** the wound
   a. reflects   b. lances   c. elevates   d. blockades   _____lances_____

4. the monks' recording of **hymns**
   a. chants   b. lances   c. blockades   d. sites   _____chants_____

5. ordered the troops to **isolate** the enemy town
   a. lance   b. despair   c. blockade   d. reflect   _____blockade_____

6. chose to work as a **preacher**
   a. blockade   b. missionary   c. lance   d. site   _____missionary_____

Antonyms

*For each item below choose the word that is most nearly **opposite** in meaning to the word or phrase in **boldface**. Then write your choice on the line provided.*

1. a **meaningful** action
   a. heroic   b. pointless   c. toxic d. extraordinary   _____pointless_____

2. a medicine that **lowers** blood pressure
   a. elevates   b. blockades   c. chants   d. reflects   _____elevates_____

3. remembered for their **cowardly** deeds
   a. missionary   b. toxic   c. pointless   d. heroic   _____heroic_____

4. **harmless** to pets
   a. pointless   b. heroic   c. toxic   d. reflected   _____toxic_____

5. materials that **absorb** sound
   a. reflect   b. blockade   c. chant   d. elevate   _____reflect_____

6. a story of **faith**
   a. blockade   b. chant   c. despair   d. site   _____despair_____

Completing the Sentence

From the list of words on pages 88–89, choose the one that best completes each item below. Then write the word in the space provided. (You may have to change the word's ending.)

FIRST AID FIRST!

■ One of the dangers of hiking or camping is snake bite. If you are bitten, it is _____**pointless**_____ to panic. There is nothing to be gained by going to pieces.

■ You need not _____**despair**_____ if you can stay calm. Rather than lose hope, the important thing is to take some simple first-aid steps.

■ Tie off the bite to keep _____**toxic**_____ fluids from traveling through your body.

■ If swelling occurs, you may have to _____**lance**_____ the bite with a clean, sharp knife. Then go immediately to the nearest doctor or hospital.

SPECIAL REWARDS

■ People who choose the life of a _____**missionary**_____ need to be strong and brave. Their choice can bring many difficulties and hardships. But it can also bring them remarkable experiences and special rewards.

■ They may travel to _____**extraordinary**_____ places that few outsiders have ever visited. They may meet people who are very different from themselves.

■ The good works of these dedicated individuals _____**reflect**_____ their wish to help others. Such a life can enrich both the helpers and those they help.

CIVIL RIGHTS FOR ALL

■ There are times when bold acts by ordinary people _____**elevate**_____ us all to new heights of justice.

■ Before the civil rights movement of the 1960s, some people set up _____**blockades**_____ to keep blacks from entering "white" schools and stores.

■ Groups that wanted to end racism got together to _____**chant**_____ sayings such as "We Shall Overcome" and "Equality Now." These people came from all walks of life, but they had the same goal: equal rights for all.

■ Lunch counters, bus stops, and schools were among the _____**sites**_____ of early civil rights struggles.

■ Thanks to the _____**heroic**_____ work of African American leaders such as Dr. Martin Luther King, Jr., and of thousands of ordinary people, racial segregation was finally outlawed.

Word Associations

*Circle the letter next to the word or expression that best completes the sentence or answers the question. Pay special attention to the word in **boldface**.*

1. A **pointless** movie would be
   a. extremely dull
   b. very long
   c. a little bit funny
   d. without meaning

2. If you make a **heroic** effort, you
   a. try everything you can
   b. think about helping
   c. give up hope
   d. wear a cape or a mask

3. If you drank a **toxic** liquid, you might
   a. sing off-key
   b. grow too big
   c. get very sick
   d. develop superhuman powers

4. The way to **lance** something is
   a. to tickle it
   b. to soak it
   c. to puncture it
   d. to ignore it

5. What might a **missionary** be likely to do?
   a. build a church
   b. read gossip magazines
   c. move to Antarctica
   d. ignore other people

6. With **extraordinary** speed, you
   a. would win most races
   b. would love to read
   c. would walk a lot
   d. would sleep late

7. If a pond **reflects** the trees around it, you can
   a. throw sticks into the water
   b. see the trees in the water
   c. throw away your mirror
   d. think about nature

8. To **elevate** your hand,
   a. hold it over your head
   b. put it in your pocket
   c. shake it back and forth
   d. wear a mitten

9. When I moved away, I **despaired**
   a. of getting any birthday cards
   b. of seeing my old friends
   c. of having enough food
   d. of finding a movie theater

10. You might **chant** if you like to
    a. take risks
    b. sing
    c. exercise
    d. watch television

11. Which is a historic **site**?
    a. President Lincoln's top hat
    b. the Stars and Stripes
    c. the White House
    d. the U.S. Constitution

12. Which might form a **blockade**?
    a. trays of ice cubes
    b. boards and bricks
    c. first-aid kits
    d. pens and pencils

UNIT 12

Definitions

Study the spelling, pronunciation, part of speech, and definition given for each of the words below. Write the word in the blank space in the sentence that follows. Then read the synonyms and antonyms.

1. **bristle**
   ('bri səl)

   (n.) a stiff, short hair or fiber
   Use a toothbrush with soft, gentle _____bristles_____.

   (v.) to have hair standing on end; to show anger; to be full of
   An insulting remark may make a person _____bristle_____ with anger.

   SYNONYMS: a whisker, spine, quill; to stiffen, rise, seethe, teem, swarm

2. **circular**
   ('sər kyə lər)

   (adj.) forming, moving, or being like a circle, round; indirect
   The _____circular_____ pathway goes around the pond.

   (n.) a leaflet or printed advertisement meant to be given to many people
   We received a _____circular_____ describing sales at the mall.

   SYNONYMS: ring-shaped, disc-shaped; roundabout; flyer, handbill, brochure
   ANTONYMS: linear, straight, direct

3. **coarse**
   (kôrs)

   (adj.) low, common, or of poor quality; made of comparatively large parts; rough to the touch; using bad manners or rude language
   Most people are offended by _____coarse_____ behavior.

   SYNONYMS: rugged, crude, harsh, grainy; scratchy; vulgar, foul, gross
   ANTONYMS: smooth, silky, delicate; gentle, refined, polite

4. **discard**
   (v., dis 'kärd;
   n., 'dis kärd)

   (v.) to get rid of or throw away
   Please _____discard_____ your newspapers into recycling bins.

   (n.) something cast off or thrown away
   Donate your clothing _____discards_____ to a charity.

   SYNONYMS: to dump, dispose of, eliminate
   ANTONYMS: to save, keep, retain

5. **extreme**
   (ik 'strēm)

   (adj.) to the highest or greatest degree; exaggerated; farthest possible
   Most people avoid _____extreme_____ heat and cold.

   (n.) the highest, farthest, or greatest; one end of a range
   Songs often describe _____extremes_____ of emotion.

   SYNONYMS: utmost, ultimate; excessive, drastic; outermost
   ANTONYMS: limited, mild, ordinary, usual; close, near

6. **focus**
   ('fō kəs)

   (n.) sharpness or clarity; the center of activity or interest
   It is easy to adjust the _____focus_____ of binoculars.

   (v.) to correct for sharpness and clarity; to concentrate
   Always take the time to _____focus_____ your camera.

   SYNONYMS: the center, heart, emphasis, direction; to direct, adjust, sharpen
   ANTONYMS: the background; to blur, ignore, neglect

7. **grasp**
   (grasp)

   (v.) to take hold with the arms or hands; to take eagerly; to understand
   A person who trips on a stairway will probably _____ **grasp** _____ *the handrail.*

   (n.) the reach of arms or hands; the power to reach or hold onto; understanding
   It's important to have a good _____ **grasp** _____ *of addition.*

   SYNONYMS: to clutch; to get; to perceive; control; perception, comprehension
   ANTONYMS: to drop, release, loosen, free, slip; to misunderstand

8. **inspire**
   (in 'spīr)

   (v.) to guide, excite, uplift, or encourage; to bring about or cause
   The Olympic Games _____ **inspire** _____ *athletes to do their best.*

   SYNONYMS: to influence, motivate, move, affect, touch, arouse, kindle, spark
   ANTONYMS: to deter, discourage

9. **magnify**
   ('mag nə fī)

   (v.) to increase in importance, exaggerate; to make bigger
   A microscope can _____ **magnify** _____ *tiny objects.*

   SYNONYMS: to intensify, increase, inflate, boost; to enlarge, expand, swell
   ANTONYMS: to diminish, reduce, lessen, shrink

10. **marine**
    (mə 'rēn)

    (adj.) related to or of the sea, sailing, or shipping; related to the seagoing branch of the armed forces
    Whales are _____ **marine** _____ *mammals, not fish.*

    (n.) a soldier who serves on a ship, a member of the U. S. Marine Corps
    _____ **Marines** _____ *have taken part in every important American naval battle since 1775.*

    SYNONYMS: nautical, maritime, oceanic, aquatic, coastal, naval
    ANTONYMS: freshwater, land

11. **quake**
    (kwāk)

    (v.) to shake or move back and forth; to tremble
    People who live in California often feel the ground _____ **quake** _____ .

    (n.) a shaking back and forth or trembling; an earthquake
    A minor _____ **quake** _____ *does little damage.*

    SYNONYMS: to shudder, shiver, vibrate, quaver; a tremor, shock

12. **troublesome**
    ('trə bəl səm)

    (adj.) difficult; causing annoyance, bother, or worry
    It is _____ **troublesome** _____ *to run out of gas on the highway.*

    SYNONYMS: hard; annoying, worrisome, bothersome, upsetting
    ANTONYMS: easy; untroubling

For each item below choose the word whose meaning is suggested by the clue given. Then write the word in the space provided.

1. When a cat crosses a dog's path, the dog's hair may _____**bristle**_____.
   a. inspire   b. focus   c. grasp   d. bristle

2. A teacher tries to encourage students and _____**inspire**_____ them to study hard.
   a. quake   b. inspire   c. bristle   d. magnify

3. If you take hold of something eagerly, you _____**grasp**_____ it.
   a. magnify   b. focus   c. grasp   d. discard

4. Silk feels smooth, but a rough fabric like burlap is _____**coarse**_____ to the touch.
   a. troublesome   b. extreme   c. circular   d. coarse

5. CDs, frisbees, and doughnuts are _____**circular**_____ in shape.
   a. circular   b. troublesome   c. coarse   d. marine

6. When you concentrate all your attention on something, you _____**focus**_____ on it.
   a. magnify   b. focus   c. grasp   d. discard

7. A VCR that is hard to use and that ruins tapes could be described as _____**troublesome**_____.
   a. troublesome   b. circular   c. marine   d. coarse

8. When the ground shakes or moves back and forth, it may be a _____**quake**_____.
   a. focus   b. discard   c. quake   d. bristle

9. Creatures that live in the ocean are _____**marine**_____ animals.
   a. circular   b. marine   c. extreme   d. troublesome

10. When you get rid of things you can no longer use, you _____**discard**_____ them.
    a. discard   b. focus   c. grasp   d. magnify

11. The very severe cold of the Antarctic winter is the most _____**extreme**_____ on Earth.
    a. coarse   b. marine   c. extreme   d. circular

12. If you make a mistake seem more serious than it is, you _____**magnify**_____ the problem.
    a. discard   b. inspire   c. bristle   d. magnify

Synonyms

For each item below choose the word that is most nearly the **same** in meaning as the word or phrase in **boldface.** Then write your choice on the line provided.

1. **shiver** in the cold wind
   a. discard   b. magnify   c. grasp   d. quake   _____quake_____

2. a very **difficult** situation
   a. coarse   b. circular   c. marine   d. troublesome   _____troublesome_____

3. **sharpened** the image on the screen
   a. inspired   b. bristled   c. discarded   d. focused   _____focused_____

4. **aroused** great loyalty among the players
   a. bristled   b. inspired   c. magnified   d. discarded   _____inspired_____

5. covered with stiff **hairs**
   a. grasps   b. circulars   c. bristles   d. quakes   _____bristles_____

6. my favorite **aquatic** sport
   a. marine   b. circular   c. coarse   d. troublesome   _____marine_____

Antonyms

For each item below choose the word that is most nearly **opposite** in meaning to the word or phrase in **boldface.** Then write your choice on the line provided.

1. **save** your ticket stub
   a. discard   b. inspire   c. magnify   d. focus   _____discard_____

2. a **polite** remark
   a. circular   b. marine   c. coarse   d. extreme   _____coarse_____

3. a **mild** winter
   a. coarse   b. extreme   c. circular   d. troublesome   _____extreme_____

4. tried to **reduce** the noise
   a. magnify   b. bristle   c. grasp   d. inspire   _____magnify_____

5. follow the **straight** path
   a. marine   b. extreme   c. coarse   d. circular   _____circular_____

6. **misunderstand** the main idea
   a. inspire   b. grasp   c. discard   d. quake   _____grasp_____

Completing the Sentence *From the list of words on pages 94–95, choose the one that best completes each item below. Then write the word in the space provided. (You may have to change the word's ending.)*

BUYER BEWARE

■ Advertisers try to _____**inspire**_____ people to buy their products. They do this by making whatever they have to sell sound appealing and necessary.

■ One way that they do this is through smart, funny ads that _____**focus**_____ your attention on a product and make you want to try it.

■ Some advertisers mail out catalogs or _____**circulars**_____ to attract customers. Many people read such ads carefully to find the best bargains.

■ But mail ads do not interest everyone. Some people think of them as junk mail and _____**discard**_____ them without even looking at them.

■ Whatever kind of ads you look at, remember that advertisers may _____**magnify**_____ their products' good points. There is plenty of truth to the old saying "Let the buyer beware."

SEEING BENEATH THE SURFACE

■ Snorkeling will do more than give you a close look at all kinds of interesting _____**marine**_____ life. It will give you an idea of what a fish sees.

■ Many colorful fish live near coral reefs. When you snorkel near a reef, you need to use _____**extreme**_____ care. Reefs are filled with living creatures, and you must avoid injuring them in any way.

■ You also need to take care that you are not injured by the corals. Many have _____**coarse**_____ surfaces that can give you a nasty scrape or cut. And some kinds of corals can sting. So be cautious when snorkeling.

YOU CAN WORK IT OUT

■ You can often solve _____**troublesome**_____ problems if you talk things out with members of your family or with friends.

■ Don't _____**quake**_____ at the idea of talking about difficult or embarrassing matters. There is really nothing to make you tremble.

■ If another person can _____**grasp**_____ what it is that is bothering you, you can work together to find a solution.

■ If you don't agree with what the other person suggests, try not to get angry and _____**bristle**_____. Explain what it is you disagree with, and keep talking.

Word Associations

*Circle the letter next to the word or expression that best completes the sentence or answers the question. Pay special attention to the word in **boldface**.*

1. **Extreme** behavior is usually
   a. excessive
   b. friendly
   c. thoughtful
   d. ordinary

2. **Troublesome** neighbors probably
   a. live across the street
   b. annoy you quite often
   c. get a lot of mail
   d. work on weekends

3. Clever inventions **inspire** me
   a. to try to build things myself
   b. to stay inside
   c. to feed the cat
   d. to get a flu shot

4. If you **grasp** a pillow, you
   a. sleep on it
   b. sew a cover for it
   c. put your arms around it
   d. store it in the attic

5. Clocks with **circular** faces
   a. look round
   b. are colorful
   c. look square
   d. are electric

6. A mirror that **magnifies** things makes them look
   a. shinier than they are
   b. flatter than they are
   c. smaller than they are
   d. bigger than they are

7. If you lived through a **quake**, you could describe how
   a. ducks stayed dry
   b. you made a quilt
   c. Earth looked to astronauts
   d. objects shook and moved

8. A hairbrush with soft **bristles**
   a. is good to paint with
   b. is too heavy to lift
   c. is too expensive
   d. is gentle on the scalp

9. If I **focus** on my homework, I
   a. can have two desserts
   b. can get a new camera
   c. can understand the lesson
   d. can play the flute

10. Which is a **marine** animal?
    a. a shark
    b. a tiger
    c. a butterfly
    d. a giraffe

11. A suit of **coarse** cloth feels
    a. silky
    b. scratchy
    c. slimy
    d. smelly

12. If I **discard** a book, I
    a. write an essay on it
    b. read it again
    c. give it away
    d. write my name in it

Unit 12 ■ 99

Selecting Word Meanings

*For each of the following items circle the choice that is most nearly the **same** in meaning as the word in **boldface.***

1. **blockade** the entry to the fort
   a. close off   b. open up   c. fill in   d. pass by

2. **discipline** the puppy
   a. forgive   b. reward   c. train   d. feed

3. **enclose** a check
   a. spend   b. open   c. cash   d. include

4. **coarse** words
   a. gentle   b. rude   c. fine   d. hoarse

5. within our **grasp**
   a. prison   b. reach   c. neighborhood   d. closet

6. a **pointless** joke
   a. meaningless   b. sensible   c. dull   d. pleasant

7. **dwell** in large groups
   a. play   b. travel   c. leave   d. live

8. a drop in **juvenile** crime
   a. adult   b. organized   c. youthful   d. violent

9. the **site** of the old barn
   a. owner   b. entrance   c. location   d. picture

10. **gradual** deepening of the water
    a. slow   b. sudden   c. dangerous   d. widespread

11. in **extreme** danger
    a. little   b. utmost   c. ordinary   d. some

12. **register** for the contest
    a. practice   b. withdraw   c. referee   d. sign up

Spelling

*For each item below study the **boldface** word in which there is a blank. If a letter is missing, fill in the blank to make a correctly spelled word. If the word is already spelled correctly, leave the blank empty.*

1. in deep **d e spair**

2. an **outs t anding** student

3. **toxi c** chemicals

4. **proceed __** to the exit

5. **tre a ty** on global warming

6. **unea s y** about the visit

7. **di s card** the envelope

8. **e a rnest** words

9. a **jag g ed** blade

10. **missi o nary** work

11. emergency **provi s ions**

12. **reflec __ t** on the past

Antonyms

*For each of the following items circle the choice that is most nearly the **opposite** in meaning to the word in **boldface**.*

1. decided to **convict** him
   a. sentence   b. judge   (c.) release   d. arrest

2. **extraordinary** deeds
   (a.) usual   b. kind   c. amazing   d. cruel

3. **unfit** for the job
   a. unqualified   b. eager   c. available   (d.) suitable

4. **nourishes** their hopes
   a. feeds   (b.) starves   c. shares   d. punishes

5. **elevate** our spirits
   a. tease   b. boost   c. require   (d.) lower

6. a **circular** route
   (a.) straight   b. roundabout   c. correct   d. unfamiliar

7. hear **distress** in her voice
   a. irritation   (b.) delight   c. grief   d. doubt

8. **troublesome** chores
   a. annoying   b. thankless   (c.) easy   d. endless

Words have been left out of the following passage. For each numbered item in the passage, fill in the circle next to the word in the margin that best fills the blank space. Then answer each question below by writing a sentence that contains one of the words you have chosen.

You have probably watched a wide __1__ of nature shows. You may have seen a plant burst into bloom or watched the slow struggle of a baby snake breaking out of its leathery egg. If you have seen such things, you have experienced the wonder of time-lapse photography.

Most of us notice big changes, but we often miss small ones. Time-lapse photography captures a(n) __2__ process that happens little by little over hours or days. Few of us would have the patience to sit still long enough to observe what a camera can record.

Time-lapse photographers __3__ a camera on one spot for many hours. They may take thousands of hours of film or videotape. During editing, they piece together the most dramatic shots and cut the ones where not much happens. The result seems to speed up time.

Choosing the right __4__ for the camera is as important for time-lapse photographers as choosing a subject. The subject will determine where the camera should be located. For a film about a storm, for example, the camera will be aimed at the wide sky. Once the camera is in place, it will record the story as it unfolds.

1. ○ grasp
   ● variety
   ○ provision
   ○ blockade

2. ○ extreme
   ○ heroic
   ○ pointless
   ● gradual

3. ○ sift
   ○ reflect
   ● focus
   ○ enclose

4. ● site
   ○ treaty
   ○ register
   ○ lance

5. What do the photographers look for when deciding where to shoot a time-lapse film?

   They look for the **site** that fits the subject they wish to film.

6. Why does time-lapse photography take place over a long time?

   Time-lapse photography captures a **gradual** process.

7. How do the photographers record this process?

   The photographers **focus** the camera on one spot for many hours.

8. How might you see examples of time-lapse photography?

   You can see examples by watching a **variety** of nature shows.

Analogies

In each of the following circle the letter for the item that best completes the comparison. Then explain the relationship on the lines provided.

1. juvenile is to **mature** as
- (a.) cowardly is to heroic
- b. earnest is to solemn
- c. fast is to quick
- d. tardy is to late

Relationship: <u>"Juvenile" and "mature" are</u> <u>antonyms/opposite in meaning; "cowardly"</u> <u>and "heroic" are antonyms/opposite</u> <u>in meaning.</u>

2. chant is to **hymn** as
- a. discipline is to disorder
- b. marine is to civilian
- (c.) grumble is to protest
- d. variety is to unity

Relationship: <u>"Chant" and "hymn" are</u> <u>synonyms/mean the same; "grumble" and</u> <u>"protest" are synonyms/mean the same.</u>

3. dungeon is to **prison** as
- a. dark is to light
- (b.) blockade is to barrier
- c. convict is to jailer
- d. despair is to hope

Relationship: <u>"Dungeon" and "prison" are</u> <u>synonyms/mean the same; "blockade"</u> <u>and "barrier" are synonyms/mean</u> <u>the same.</u>

4. bristle is to **stiff** as
- a. pillow is to hard
- b. glass is to soft
- c. sandpaper is to smooth
- (d.) lance is to sharp

Relationship: <u>**A bristle may be described**</u> <u>**as stiff; a lance may be described as sharp.**</u>

Challenge: Make up your own

Write a comparison using the words in the box below. (Hint: There are three possible analogies.)
Then write the relationship on the lines provided.

toxic	computer	safe	shrink
chair	magnify	camera	car
vehicle	lens	screen	furniture

Analogy: _____ is to _____ as _____ is to _____.

Relationship: <u>**See Table of Contents**</u>

_____

Word Families

*The words in **boldface** in the sentences below are related to words introduced in Units 9–12. For example, the nouns enclosure and procedure in item 1 are related to the verbs proceed (Unit 10) and enclose (Unit 9). Based on your understanding of the unit words that follow, circle the related word in **boldface** that best completes each sentence.*

circular	discipline	distress	drench	dwell
elevate	enclose	extreme	earnest	heroic
inspire	magnify	nourish	proceed	reflect
register	tardy	toxic	uneasy	variety

1. The zoo recently built an air-conditioned (**enclosure**/**procedure**) for its polar bears.

2. It is the principal's job to take (**varietal**/**disciplinary**) action when students are unruly.

3. A homeless family's greatest need is a (**dwelling**/**magnification**).

4. The President presented the pilots with medals for their (**uneasiness**/ **heroism**) during the rescue mission.

5. It was so cold that we had no feeling in our (**extremities**/**tardiness**).

6. The (**gradualness**/**pointlessness**) of the speaker's jokes annoyed the audience.

7. (**Registration**/**Elevation**) forms for summer camp must be completed by the end of March.

8. The veterinarian said that the stray cat we found needed lots of (**earnestness**/**nourishment**).

9. The Nobel Prize winner's (**inspirational**/**distressing**) speech restored our hope for the future.

10. The safest toys for young children are made of (**nontoxic**/**semicircular**) materials.

Use the clues below to complete the crossword puzzle.
(All of the answers are words from Units 9–12.)

```
 1               2
 F  O  C  U  S
             P
       3
       G  R  A  S  P
 4           E
 Q
 5     6                    7
 D  U  N  G  E  O  N        V
    A     R           8     A
    K     U           D     R
    E     M     9     I     I
10       11 S           S
 T        B  R  I  S  T  L  E
    R     L     F     R  12
13                       T  A  R  D  Y
 R  E  F  L  E  C  T     E  Y
    A                    S
14
 T  R  O  U  B  L  E  S  O  M  E
    Y
```

Across
1. to concentrate
3. to clutch or seize
5. an underground prison

11.

12. late
13. to throw back
14. annoying

Down
2. a splurge or binge
4. to tremble
6. a muttered complaint
7. a lack of sameness
8. to make unhappy
9. to put through a strainer
10. a settlement or pact

Definitions

Study the spelling, pronunciation, part of speech, and definition given for each of the words below. Write the word in the blank space in the sentence that follows. Then read the synonyms and antonyms.

1. **abstract**
   (ab 'strakt)

   (adj.) having to do with an idea or quality rather than an object; hard to understand; (in art) with little likeness to real people or things
   A character in a book may stand for an _____**abstract**_____ *idea such as kindness.*

   SYNONYMS: conceptual, theoretical; obscure; a summary
   ANTONYMS: actual, physical, real, concrete; realistic

2. **ally**
   (v., ə 'lī;
   n., 'a lī)

   (v.) to unite or join for a special purpose
   Parents may _____**ally**_____ *themselves with teachers to tutor students who need extra help.*

   (n.) a person or country joined with another for a special purpose
   Great Britain was an _____**ally**_____ *of the United States in World War II.*

   SYNONYMS: to unite, associate, combine; a partner, associate
   ANTONYMS: an enemy, opponent

3. **appoint**
   (ə 'point)

   (v.) to choose (someone) for a position or duty; to decide on
   It is the responsibility of the mayor to _____**appoint**_____ *a police chief.*

   SYNONYMS: to designate, assign, elect
   ANTONYMS: to dismiss, remove, suspend

4. **attentive**
   (ə 'ten tiv)

   (adj.) paying attention; thoughtful and polite
   When you write a composition, you should be _____**attentive**_____ *to spelling and punctuation.*

   SYNONYMS: observant, alert; considerate, courteous
   ANTONYMS: inattentive, unobservant; inconsiderate

5. **bonus**
   ('bō nəs)

   (n.) something extra or beyond what is owed or expected
   Many companies give their employees a _____**bonus**_____ *at the end of the year.*

   SYNONYMS: an addition, reward, benefit, gift, prize
   ANTONYMS: a penalty, deduction, fine

6. **carefree**
   ('kâr frē)

   (adj.) without troubles, worries, or responsibilities
   Summer vacation is usually a _____**carefree**_____ *time.*

   SYNONYMS: untroubled, lighthearted
   ANTONYMS: troubled, worried, anxious

Assembly lines are still used in the **manufacture** (word 8) of automobiles but many jobs once performed by people are now done by robotic machines.

7. **courtesy**
   ('kər tə sē)

   (n.) polite, thoughtful, or considerate behavior; a polite act; a favor
   Customers appreciate being treated with _____courtesy_____.

   SYNONYMS: care, concern, regard, politeness, thoughtfulness
   ANTONYMS: discourtesy, disregard, rudeness

8. **manufacture**
   (man yə 'fak chər)

   (v.) to make something, especially using machinery; to make up
   I had to _____manufacture_____ an excuse.

   (n.) the making of something, especially using machinery
   A factory in our town specializes in the _____manufacture_____ of furniture.

   SYNONYMS: to assemble, construct, build, produce; to invent, concoct

9. **mistrust**
   (mis 'trəst)

   (n.) a lack of confidence
   Some people have a deep _____mistrust_____ of politicians.

   (v.) to have no confidence in; to be suspicious of; to doubt
   Sometimes I _____mistrust_____ my own judgment.

   SYNONYMS: doubt, uncertainty, suspicion; to question, disbelieve
   ANTONYMS: trust, confidence, belief; to trust, believe

10. **noticeable**
    ('nō tə sə bəl)

    (adj.) easy to see; likely to be observed; worthy of attention
    We saw a _____noticeable_____ improvement in their play.

    SYNONYMS: observable, visible, obvious, evident
    ANTONYMS: overlooked, hidden, obscure

11. **overthrow**
    (ō vər 'thrō)

    (v.) to overturn; to bring about the fall or end of
    The rebels will _____overthrow_____ the cruel ruler.

    (n.) an act of bringing down; defeat
    The people celebrated the _____overthrow_____ of the heartless king.

    SYNONYMS: to remove, bring down, topple, destroy, ruin, upset; collapse, ruin
    ANTONYMS: to preserve, support, restore

12. **peculiar**
    (pi 'kyül yər)

    (adj.) not like the normal or usual; odd or curious; belonging to a particular group, person, place, or thing
    Everyone is talking about the _____peculiar_____ weather this year.

    SYNONYMS: special, particular, bizarre, unusual, strange, distinctive, unique
    ANTONYMS: ordinary, routine, regular, normal, common

Match the Meaning

For each item below choose the word whose meaning is suggested by the clue given. Then write the word in the space provided.

1. Our advisor can _____**appoint**_____ a leader for our debating team.
   a. overthrow   b. manufacture   c. abstract   d. appoint

2. To bring about the end of something is to _____**overthrow**_____ it.
   a. mistrust   b. overthrow   c. appoint   d. manufacture

3. If you do not have confidence in something, you _____**mistrust**_____ it.
   a. appoint   b. ally   c. mistrust   d. manufacture

4. Something that is unusual or odd is _____**peculiar**_____.
   a. attentive   b. abstract   c. carefree   d. peculiar

5. If something is easy to see, it is _____**noticeable**_____.
   a. noticeable   b. abstract   c. attentive   d. carefree

6. When you get a free gift with a subscription, you get a(n) _____**bonus**_____.
   a. abstract   b. bonus   c. ally   d. manufacture

7. Speakers appreciate audiences that are _____**attentive**_____.
   a. attentive   b. abstract   c. carefree   d. peculiar

8. To be kind or polite to other people is to behave with _____**courtesy**_____.
   a. mistrust   b. manufacture   c. courtesy   d. bonus

9. A person who feels _____**carefree**_____ does not worry.
   a. noticeable   b. carefree   c. peculiar   d. attentive

10. The workers in a factory _____**manufacture**_____ products.
    a. manufacture   b. abstract   c. mistrust   d. appoint

11. Something that is about ideas and qualities rather than people is _____**abstract**_____.
    a. attentive   b. carefree   c. abstract   d. noticeable

12. You may _____**ally**_____ yourself with others to improve your community.
    a. ally   b. overthrow   c. appoint   d. mistrust

Synonyms

*For each item below choose the word that is most nearly the **same** in meaning as the word or phrase in **boldface**. Then write your choice on the line provided.*

1. **doubted** the evidence
   a. mistrusted   b. overthrew   c. appointed   d. manufactured   _____mistrusted_____

2. received an unexpected **reward**
   a. overthrow   b. ally   c. manufacture   d. bonus   _____bonus_____

3. **produce** lawn mowers
   a. manufacture   b. abstract   c. mistrust   d. appoint   _____manufacture_____

4. **topple** a government
   a. appoint   b. overthrow   c. mistrust   d. manufacture   _____overthrow_____

5. faithful **supporters**
   a. abstracts   b. allies   c. bonuses   d. courtesies   _____allies_____

6. walked with a **distinct** limp
   a. attentive   b. carefree   c. noticeable   d. peculiar   _____noticeable_____

Antonyms

*For each item below choose the word that is most nearly **opposite** in meaning to the word or phrase in **boldface**. Then write your choice on the line provided.*

1. **anxious** tourists
   a. attentive   b. carefree   c. noticeable   d. peculiar   _____carefree_____

2. **neglectful** waiters
   a. abstract   b. peculiar   c. carefree   d. attentive   _____attentive_____

3. frightened by **ordinary** noises
   a. attentive   b. abstract   c. peculiar   d. noticeable   _____peculiar_____

4. **realistic** paintings
   a. abstract   b. noticeable   c. carefree   d. attentive   _____abstract_____

5. show **rudeness** to others
   a. overthrow   b. mistrust   c. bonus   d. courtesy   _____courtesy_____

6. **dismiss** the commander
   a. overthrow   b. appoint   c. ally   d. manufacture   _____appoint_____

Completing the Sentence

From the list of words on pages 106–107, choose the one that best completes each item below. Write the word in the space provided. (You may have to change the word's ending.)

PAYING ATTENTION

■ A guest speaker visited our science class last week. We were on our best behavior and tried to be ____**attentive**____ during the talk.

■ The speaker discussed many ____**abstract**____ ideas about time and space that were very hard to understand.

■ To make things more difficult, the speaker's voice had a(n) ____**peculiar**____ singsong tone that was distracting.

■ We applauded our guest politely, but some students gave a(n) ____**noticeable**____ sigh of relief when the speech ended.

NOW THAT'S JUSTICE!

■ In 1967, President Lyndon Johnson ____**appointed**____ Thurgood Marshall to be the first African American to serve on the Supreme Court.

■ For many years Marshall had been a lawyer for the National Association for the Advancement of Colored People (NAACP). During those years he had argued more than thirty cases before the Supreme Court. Many of these cases helped to ____**overthrow**____ laws that had discriminated against African Americans.

■ At first some people ____**mistrusted**____ Marshall and opposed his nomination.

■ But Marshall's ____**allies**____ supported him, and he took his place on the Court. He went on to become one of America's greatest justices.

THE BUSINESS OF PLAY

■ A lot of people think it must be fun to work in a toy factory. They would probably be surprised to learn that the ____**manufacture**____ of toys is not a game.

■ You may think of toys in connection with ____**carefree**____ play, but to toy companies they are serious business.

■ In some factories bosses offer cash ____**bonuses**____ to workers who suggest ways to speed up production.

■ Owners of toy stores often get samples of new toys as a ____**courtesy**____. In return for the favor, the owners may test the toys with their customers and then tell the companies how well the toys are liked.

Word Associations

*Circle the letter next to the word or expression that best completes the sentence or answers the question. Pay special attention to the word in **boldface**.*

1. Which is **abstract**?
   a. water
   b. food
   c. thought
   d. metal

2. I might **mistrust** a TV ad that
   a. does not give me any facts
   b. is on after midnight
   c. uses actors and costumes
   d. raises honest questions

3. The President may **appoint**
   a. starting pitchers
   b. your town's mayor
   c. talk show hosts
   d. cabinet members

4. A **noticeable** difference may be
   a. hard to see
   b. hard to describe
   c. confusing to someone
   d. obvious to everyone

5. Which might **carefree** people do?
   a. worry about everything
   b. argue with their friends
   c. whistle their favorite tunes
   d. work on their homework

6. A **peculiar** outfit is one that is
   a. expensive
   b. strange
   c. ragged
   d. colorful

7. Which may be **overthrown**?
   a. kings and queens
   b. salt and pepper
   c. shoes and socks
   d. dogs and cats

8. Someone who is your **ally** will
   a. gossip about you
   b. be on your side
   c. borrow your books
   d. ignore you

9. I get a **bonus** from my book club
   a. if I order lots of books
   b. if I ask nicely for one
   c. if I break my leg
   d. if I owe it lots of money

10. If you **manufacture** excuses, you
    a. open a factory
    b. buy them at a discount
    c. think them up yourself
    d. tell the truth

11. Which comment shows **courtesy**?
    a. "Who asked you?"
    b. "That's not a good plan."
    c. "Get out of my way!"
    d. "May I serve you more soup?"

12. You'll be more **attentive** if you
    a. listen or look closely
    b. take attendance
    c. install a smoke alarm
    d. curl up on the couch

Definitions

Study the spelling, pronunciation, part of speech, and definition given for each of the words below. Write the word in the blank space in the sentence that follows. Then read the synonyms and antonyms.

1. **absolute**
   ('ab sə lüt)

   (adj.) without flaws or imperfections; without limits; without doubt
   The witness swore to tell the _____**absolute**_____ *truth.*

   SYNONYMS: pure, perfect; entire, whole, complete, unlimited; certain, sure
   ANTONYMS: flawed; limited, incomplete, restricted; uncertain

2. **arena**
   (ə 'rē nə)

   (n.) an enclosed space used for sports or shows; a field of interest, activity, conflict, or debate
   The senator has been in the political _____**arena**_____ *ever since she was elected president of her high school class.*

   SYNONYMS: a stadium, theater, auditorium; field, scene

3. **compliment**
   ('käm plə mənt)

   (n.) a remark or action that shows admiration, praise, or approval; (used in the plural) good wishes
   Everyone likes to receive a _____**compliment**_____ .

   (v.) to give praise or admiration to
   The losing team _____**compliments**_____ *the winners on their victory.*

   SYNONYMS: congratulations; regards; to flatter, applaud, salute
   ANTONYMS: blame, criticism; to insult, denounce, criticize

4. **deliberate**
   (v., di 'li bə rāt;
   adj., di 'li bə rət)

   (v.) to think about or discuss very carefully
   A jury may _____**deliberate**_____ *for days before reaching a verdict.*
   (adj.) done or said on purpose; careful; at a slow pace
   A person may tell a _____**deliberate**_____ *lie to avoid blame.*

   SYNONYMS: to consider, debate, weigh; intentional; careful, thoughtful, purposeful
   ANTONYMS: unwitting, impulsive; careless, haphazard, hasty, hurried

5. **dense**
   (dens)

   (adj.) close or packed together; thick; stupid
   A _____**dense**_____ *crowd blocked the entrance to the building.*

   SYNONYMS: compact, solid, crowded; dull-witted, thickheaded
   ANTONYMS: sparse, open, scattered, thin; alert, clever, smart

6. **dominant**
   ('dä mə nənt)

   (adj.) above all others; leading or controlling; having the most power
   The President is usually the _____**dominant**_____ *figure in his or her political party.*

   SYNONYMS: chief, main, first, foremost; commanding, controlling
   ANTONYMS: inferior, secondary; humble, modest

Hazardous (word 7) waste can cause serious damage to the environment and health problems for people exposed to it.

7. **hazardous**
('ha zər dəs)

(adj.) involving risk or danger
Special containers are used for disposing of _____hazardous_____ waste.
SYNONYMS: dangerous, perilous, risky, unsafe
ANTONYMS: safe, certain, secure

8. **huddle**
('hə dəl)

(v.) to crowd close together; to form a closely packed group; to get together to discuss something
Campers may _____huddle_____ around a fire on a cold night.
(n.) a tightly packed group; a meeting or discussion; in football, a quick meeting of players on the field to plan the next play
The coaches held a brief _____huddle_____ on the sidelines.
SYNONYMS: to bunch, cluster, crowd; to gather; a bunch, conference

9. **necessity**
(ni 'se sə tē)

(n.) something that cannot be avoided or done without; great need
Water is a _____necessity_____ for life.
SYNONYMS: a requirement, essential, must; want
ANTONYMS: an option, extra, luxury

10. **offend**
(ə 'fend)

(v.) to break a law or rule; to cause hurt feelings, anger, or injury
Thoughtless behavior will _____offend_____ most people.
SYNONYMS: to embarrass, displease, insult, upset, irritate, annoy, wound
ANTONYMS: to please, charm, soothe

11. **regain**
(rē 'gān)

(v.) to get back; to reach again
It takes time to _____regain_____ your strength after an illness.
SYNONYM: to recover
ANTONYMS: to lose, forfeit

12. **thorough**
('thər ō)

(adj.) carried out to completion; complete in every detail; extremely careful or exact
The dentist gave me a _____thorough_____ checkup.
SYNONYMS: exhaustive, extensive, total, full
ANTONYMS: incomplete, partial, limited, unfinished; cursory, inadequate

113

Match the Meaning

For each item below choose the word whose meaning is suggested by the clue given. Then write the word in the space provided.

1. To think carefully about something is to _____**deliberate**_____.
   a. offend   b. compliment   c. regain   d. deliberate

2. When people say things that hurt your feelings, they _____**offend**_____ you.
   a. huddle   b. offend   c. deliberate   d. compliment

3. A group of people crowded close together is a(n) _____**huddle**_____.
   a. necessity   b. arena   c. huddle   d. compliment

4. For spring cleaning to be _____**thorough**_____, it should be done room by room.
   a. dense   b. dominant   c. absolute   d. thorough

5. Skating on thin ice is _____**hazardous**_____.
   a. hazardous   b. thorough   c. deliberate   d. dominant

6. A(n) _____**arena**_____ is an indoor space used for sports or shows.
   a. huddle   b. arena   c. necessity   d. compliment

7. When you get back something you have lost, you _____**regain**_____ it.
   a. compliment   b. deliberate   c. regain   d. offend

8. A fog that you cannot see through may be described as _____**dense**_____.
   a. dense   b. absolute   c. dominant   d. thorough

9. Power that has no limits is _____**absolute**_____ power.
   a. deliberate   b. dense   c. absolute   d. hazardous

10. The member of a group who has the most influence and control is the
    _____**dominant**_____ individual.
    a. absolute   b. dominant   c. thorough   d. dense

11. When someone pays me a(n) _____**compliment**_____, I feel proud and happy.
    a. compliment   b. arena   c. huddle   d. necessity

12. A(n) _____**necessity**_____ is something that you cannot do without.
    a. huddle   b. compliment   c. arena   d. necessity

Synonyms

*For each item below choose the word that is most nearly the **same** in meaning as the word or phrase in **boldface.** Then write your choice on the line provided.*

1. **crowd** under the umbrella
   a. huddle   b. regain   c. deliberate   d. compliment   _____huddle_____

2. attended a game at the county **auditorium**
   a. huddle   b. necessity   c. compliment   d. arena   _____arena_____

3. **congratulate** the winner of the scholarship
   a. compliment b. offend   c. regain   d. deliberate   _____compliment_____

4. **displeased** the audience
   a. deliberated b. offended   c. regained   d. complimented   _____offended_____

5. one of the **requirements** for the job
   a. arenas   b. necessities c. huddles   d. compliments   _____necessities_____

6. a **dangerous** path
   a. dense   b. dominant   c. hazardous   d. thorough   _____hazardous_____

Antonyms

*For each item below choose the word that is most nearly **opposite** in meaning to the word or phrase in **boldface.** Then write your choice on the line provided.*

1. a **secondary** share of the market
   a. dense   b. hazardous   c. dominant   d. thorough   _____dominant_____

2. flew through **thin** clouds
   a. absolute   b. dense   c. deliberate   d. hazardous   _____dense_____

3. did an **incomplete** job
   a. dense   b. hazardous   c. thorough   d. dominant   _____thorough_____

4. **lose** control of the vehicle
   a. compliment b. deliberate   c. offend   d. regain   _____regain_____

5. have **limited** control
   a. absolute   b. dense   c. hazardous   d. deliberate   _____absolute_____

6. at a **hurried** pace
   a. dense   b. absolute   c. deliberate   d. dominant   _____deliberate_____

Completing the Sentence

From the list of words on pages 112–113, choose the one that best completes each item below. Write the word in the space provided. (You may have to change the word's ending.)

UP, UP, AND AWAY

■ Flying a hot-air balloon is an exciting experience. But if you do not use good sense and follow proper safety precautions, it can also be _____**hazardous**_____ .

■ Clear, calm weather and open airspace are _____**necessities**_____ for safe balloon travel.

■ Darkness, bad weather, or _____**dense**_____ fog can hide dangers, such as trees, wires, and buildings.

CHESS, ANYONE?

■ In the _____**arena**_____ of strategy games, chess has many devoted fans. Chess is one of the most ancient games in the field, dating back to at least the sixth century.

■ Once chess was a favored game of the royal and the rich. Today, however, it is enjoyed by people from all walks of life. When skilled players compete at outdoor tables in city parks, spectators _____**huddle**_____ around to watch them.

■ The game's _____**dominant**_____ players stun their opponents with unexpected moves. Some of these top players have even tried their skills against those of a computer.

■ Players use clocks to limit the time they may _____**deliberate**_____ between moves.

■ A chess game may end with a narrow win or a draw. But some matches finish with one player achieving a(n) _____**absolute**_____ , flawless victory.

APOLOGY ACCEPTED

■ The other day I made a serious mistake. Without thinking, I made an unkind remark that _____**offended**_____ my best friend.

■ When I saw the hurt look on her face, I felt ashamed of myself. All I wanted was to _____**regain**_____ her trust.

■ I offered a sincere and _____**thorough**_____ apology. I also promised her that I would be more considerate of her feelings from now on.

■ My friend _____**complimented**_____ me for admitting my mistake and then forgave me. I am so glad we are best friends again!

*Circle the letter next to the word or expression that best completes the sentence or answers the question. Pay special attention to the word in **boldface**.*

1. If you **regain** the lead, you get
   a. a flashlight
   b. the daily paper
   c. a free movie ticket
   d. back in first place

2. Why might a group of people form a **huddle**?
   a. to drink hot cocoa
   b. to do laundry
   c. to talk things over
   d. to catch a fish

3. Toys **hazardous** to a baby might
   a. have floppy ears
   b. have sharp edges
   c. have cute faces
   d. have orange fur

4. When I go at a **deliberate** speed,
   a. I walk slowly
   b. I think too much
   c. I ride in a taxi cab
   d. I deserve a speeding ticket

5. A **dominant** person
   a. sings and dances
   b. eats and drinks
   c. leads and controls
   d. laughs and cries

6. A **thorough** report should include
   a. every detail
   b. spelling mistakes
   c. graphs and charts
   d. an E-mail address

7. Which is a true **necessity**?
   a. talking on the telephone
   b. sleeping ten hours a night
   c. showering every day
   d. having food and shelter

8. I might **offend** you if I asked
   a. "How about some milk?"
   b. "How silly can you be?"
   c. "Shall we sit together?"
   d. "What time is it?"

9. We might go to an **arena** to see
   a. a menu
   b. an encyclopedia
   c. a dentist
   d. a hockey game

10. With **absolute** proof, there is no
    a. evidence
    b. music
    c. doubt
    d. hot water

11. If I want to pay you a **compliment**, I might say
    a. "Nice outfit!"
    b. "That's a terrible plan!"
    c. "Good grief!"
    d. "Not on your life!"

12. A forest that is **dense** is
    a. green
    b. thick
    c. nearby
    d. far away

Study the spelling, pronunciation, part of speech, and definition given for each of the words below. Write the word in the blank space in the sentence that follows. Then read the synonyms and antonyms.

1. **adopt**
   (ə 'däpt)

   (v.) to take another person's child into one's family; to use as one's own; to accept or approve

   A family may _____ adopt _____ an orphan from a war-torn country.

   SYNONYMS: to choose, select; to endorse, approve, assume
   ANTONYMS: to reject, disown, refuse, renounce, abandon, desert

2. **agile**
   ('a jəl)

   (adj.) capable of moving easily, quickly, and gracefully; mentally quick

   Squirrels are _____ agile _____ climbers.

   SYNONYMS: nimble, spry, limber; alert, sharp
   ANTONYMS: clumsy, heavy; slow

3. **analyze**
   ('a nəl īz)

   (v.) to study the parts of something in order to understand what it is, how it is put together, or how it works; to study carefully or in detail

   Scientists _____ analyze _____ moon rocks to learn more about what the moon is made of.

   SYNONYMS: to examine, inspect, investigate, evaluate, test; to dissect

4. **assist**
   (ə 'sist)

   (v.) to give help or support

   Several doctors may _____ assist _____ a surgeon during an operation.

   (n.) the act of helping; in sports, an action that helps a teammate score or get a player out

   A hockey player may receive credit for an _____ assist _____.

   SYNONYMS: to help, aid, boost, contribute
   ANTONYMS: to hamper, hinder, obstruct; an obstruction

5. **babble**
   ('ba bəl)

   (v.) to talk foolishly or too much; to make meaningless sounds; to make a gurgling sound

   Some people can _____ babble _____ on the telephone for hours.

   (n.) a mix of meaningless sounds, usually as made by water

   The soft _____ babble _____ of a creek can be very relaxing.

   SYNONYMS: to chatter, jabber, prattle, gab; drivel, nonsense, murmur

6. **captivity**
   (kap 'ti və tē)

   (n.) the state of being confined or held against one's will

   Some prisoners of war have been held in _____ captivity _____ for years.

   SYNONYMS: slavery, confinement, custody, restraint, imprisonment, bondage
   ANTONYMS: freedom, liberty, independence

To be a successful rock climber it helps to be strong and **agile** (word 2).

7. **drab**
   (drab)

   (n.) an olive brown or brownish gray color
   The old canvas tents were a faded _____drab_____.

   (adj.) marked by dullness; like the color drab; cheerless
   A good book is good company on a _____drab_____ and rainy afternoon.

   SYNONYMS: brownish; dull, dingy, colorless, uninteresting, lackluster; dreary
   ANTONYMS: colorful, cheerful, bright

8. **fatal**
   ('fā təl)

   (adj.) causing death, destruction, or ruin
   One passenger suffered a _____fatal_____ injury.

   SYNONYMS: deadly, lethal, disastrous; decisive, fateful
   ANTONYMS: harmless, healthful

9. **generosity**
   (je nə 'rä sə tē)

   (n.) the quality of being charitable to others in thought or action; willingness to give; an act of giving
   The heiress is well known for her _____generosity_____.

   SYNONYMS: charity, unselfishness
   ANTONYMS: stinginess, cheapness, greed

10. **genuine**
    ('jen yə wən)

    (adj.) real, actually being what something appears to be; true or reliable; sincere or honest
    I found a _____genuine_____ fossil in my yard.

    SYNONYMS: authentic, original, actual; valid; trustworthy, earnest, frank
    ANTONYMS: fake, false, artificial, unreal; insincere, phony, pretended

11. **illegal**
    (i 'lē gəl)

    (adj.) against the law; against the rules
    Stealing is an _____illegal_____ act.

    SYNONYMS: unlawful, criminal, outlawed; forbidden, prohibited
    ANTONYMS: legal, lawful, allowed

12. **merit**
    ('mer ət)

    (n.) the fact of deserving something; a quality that deserves reward or praise; worth or value
    Her science project has great _____merit_____.

    (v.) to deserve, be worthy of
    His poems _____merit_____ being published.

    SYNONYMS: excellence, virtue, quality, worthiness; to earn, justify, rate
    ANTONYMS: disgrace, dishonor, failing, shortcoming, defect, flaw, fault

Match the Meaning

For each item below choose the word whose meaning is suggested by the clue given. Then write the word in the space provided.

1. If your work has _____ merit _____, it deserves praise or reward.
   a. generosity   b. babble   c. captivity   d. merit

2. To _____ adopt _____ a pet is to care for it as part of one's family.
   a. analyze   b. adopt   c. merit   d. assist

3. When I talk foolishly or too much, I _____ babble _____.
   a. adopt   b. assist   c. babble   d. analyze

4. Fabric that is _____ drab _____ is neither colorful nor cheery.
   a. illegal   b. genuine   c. agile   d. drab

5. Something that causes death is _____ fatal _____.
   a. fatal   b. drab   c. illegal   d. genuine

6. People in _____ captivity _____ are held against their will.
   a. babble   b. captivity   c. drab   d. generosity

7. A(n) _____ illegal _____ action is against the law or the rules.
   a. illegal   b. agile   c. genuine   d. fatal

8. Someone who has a(n) _____ agile _____ mind is quick and sharp.
   a. drab   b. illegal   c. agile   d. genuine

9. If something is _____ genuine _____, it is truly what it appears to be.
   a. fatal   b. genuine   c. drab   d. agile

10. When you help someone, you _____ assist _____ that person.
    a. assist   b. adopt   c. babble   d. analyze

11. When I study how something is put together, I _____ analyze _____ it.
    a. assist   b. merit   c. analyze   d. adopt

12. _____ Generosity _____ is a willingness to give to others.
    a. Babble   b. Merit   c. Captivity   d. Generosity

For each item below choose the word that is most nearly the **same** in meaning as the word or phrase in **boldface**. Then write your choice on the line provided.

1. **examine** our mistakes
   a. merit   b. analyze   c. babble   d. assist   _____ analyze

2. **chatters** about nothing
   a. babbles   b. assists   c. merits   d. adopts   _____ babbles

3. suffered in **bondage**
   a. merit   b. generosity   c. babble   d. captivity   _____ captivity

4. an idea of little or no **value**
   a. assist   b. babble   c. merit   d. generosity   _____ merit

5. an **authentic** Civil War sword
   a. genuine   b. illegal   c. drab   d. agile   _____ genuine

6. a **deadly** poison
   a. illegal   b. genuine   c. fatal   d. drab   _____ fatal

Antonyms

For each item below choose the word that is most nearly **opposite** in meaning to the word or phrase in **boldface**. Then write your choice on the line provided.

1. **hindered** the investigation
   a. assisted   b. adopted   c. merited   d. analyzed   _____ assisted

2. **abandoned** the puppy
   a. analyzed   b. assisted   c. adopted   d. merited   _____ adopted

3. a **lawful** act
   a. agile   b. illegal   c. genuine   d. drab   _____ illegal

4. wore **colorful** costumes
   a. illegal   b. fatal   c. drab   d. genuine   _____ drab

5. famous for their **cheapness**
   a. generosity   b. captivity   c. merit   d. babble   _____ generosity

6. **clumsy** mountain goats
   a. fatal   b. illegal   c. drab   d. agile   _____ agile

Completing the Sentence

From the list of words on pages 118–119, choose the one that best completes each item below. Write the word in the space provided. (You may have to change the word's ending.)

From the list of words on pages 118–119

A YEARLY EVENT

■ Each year our town holds a fall festival. It is lively and noisy and fun for everyone. But the _____ **babble** _____ of the crowd quiets down when it comes time for the mayor's ceremony.

■ The highlight of this ceremony is the announcement of the two people who _____ **merit** _____ the Best Neighbor Award.

■ This award is given to people for outstanding _____ **generosity** _____ to fellow citizens who are in need.

■ You can see the _____ **genuine** _____ delight on the winners' faces when the mayor hands them big silver keys to the city.

CLUES TO POLLUTION

■ You may think that the mud on a riverbank looks _____ **drab** _____ and ordinary. But scientists know that even though it looks dull, it may contain clues to pollution.

■ Scientists can _____ **analyze** _____ the mud to find out if any harmful chemicals are present in the soil and water.

■ This is one way that scientists can tell if there has been _____ **illegal** _____ dumping of waste materials.

■ The data scientists gather from the mud can _____ **assist** _____ them in finding and stopping the polluters.

DON'T TRY THIS AT HOME

■ Baby animals are cute. A bear cub may look so cuddly that you might think it would be fun to _____ **adopt** _____ one.

■ It is important to remember that a wild animal can be dangerous. To try to raise one in your home could be a(n) _____ **fatal** _____ mistake.

■ As the playful cub grows more _____ **agile** _____ and strong, it soon becomes too big and dangerous to be a family pet.

■ Then you would have to find a home for the animal in a zoo. You couldn't just set the bear free in a forest. A wild animal raised in _____ **captivity** _____ may not have the skills it would need to survive in the wild.

Word Associations

*Circle the letter next to the word or expression that best completes the sentence or answers the question. Pay special attention to the word in **boldface**.*

1. I **babble** when I get too
   a. excited
   b. bored
   c. angry
   d. serious

2. A **drab** outfit would be
   a. colorless or dull
   b. too small or too big
   c. made of scratchy cloth
   d. out of fashion

3. It is **illegal** to use
   a. pay telephones
   b. fake money
   c. common sense
   d. pencils

4. You would **merit** a raise if your boss
   a. owned the business
   b. knew your name
   c. thought you did poor work
   d. thought you did great work

5. A person who is **genuine** is
   a. cheerful
   b. nervous
   c. sincere
   d. clumsy

6. You can show **generosity** by
   a. opening a bank account
   b. exercising every day
   c. doing your homework
   d. sharing your lunch

7. Which might be **fatal** if eaten?
   a. applesauce
   b. drain cleaner
   c. stale crackers
   d. hot peppers

8. The state **adopts** a law if the
   a. children need parents
   b. governor takes in a family
   c. lawmakers approve it
   d. lawmakers reject it

9. You would find animals in **captivity**
   a. in the wild
   b. up a tree
   c. free to come and go
   d. in a zoo

10. When I want to **assist** someone, I will ask
    a. "May I be of help?"
    b. "Can't you do it yourself?"
    c. "What time is it?"
    d. "Do I have to?"

11. Having an **agile** mind helps you
    a. to do cartwheels
    b. to take a nap
    c. to feed your pet
    d. to catch on quickly

12. If you **analyze** a song, you'll find
    a. dots and dashes
    b. bells and whistles
    c. rhythms and melodies
    d. bones and muscles

UNIT 16

Definitions

Study the spelling, pronunciation, part of speech, and definition given for each of the words below. Write the word in the blank space in the sentence that follows. Then read the synonyms and antonyms.

1. **adorn**
   (ə 'dôrn)

   (v.) to add to the appearance of, especially with pretty objects; to dress up
   Fresh flowers and beautiful linens _____adorn_____ the dining room table.

   SYNONYMS: to decorate, ornament, enrich, grace, beautify, enhance
   ANTONYMS: to damage, mar, blemish

2. **appropriate**
   (*v.,* ə 'prō prē āt;
   adj., ə 'prō prē ət)

   (v.) to take over or use as one's own, often without permission; to set apart for a certain purpose
   A brother or sister may _____appropriate_____ your favorite book.
   (adj.) suitable or fitting
   It is _____appropriate_____ to wear a warm hat in the winter.

   SYNONYMS: to seize, confiscate, steal; to allot; correct, suitable, proper
   ANTONYMS: unfitting, unsuitable, inappropriate, improper

3. **assemble**
   (ə 'sem bəl)

   (v.) to meet or bring together; to put or fit parts together
   On Thanksgiving family members _____assemble_____ to enjoy a holiday feast.

   SYNONYMS: to convene, gather, congregate; to build, construct, join, connect
   ANTONYMS: to scatter, break up, disperse; to separate, divide

4. **colossal**
   (kə 'lä səl)

   (adj.) amazingly large, great, or powerful in size or degree
   Whale watchers hope for a glimpse of a _____colossal_____ blue whale.

   SYNONYMS: enormous, huge, gigantic, massive, immense
   ANTONYMS: tiny, small, little

5. **effective**
   (i 'fek tiv)

   (adj.) producing a desired or conclusive result; having a strong impact; starting as of a particular date or time
   The team that makes the most _____effective_____ presentation will win the debate.

   SYNONYMS: capable, potent, impressive, striking, compelling; starting, beginning
   ANTONYMS: ineffective, futile, useless, weak

6. **frail**
   (frāl)

   (adj.) weak or lacking strength; likely to give in to temptation
   Our class project is to send cheerful greeting cards to children who are in _____frail_____ health.

   SYNONYMS: delicate, feeble, sickly, slight, fragile, flimsy, brittle, breakable
   ANTONYMS: sturdy, robust, hardy, healthy; firm, strong, solid

124

This **colossal** (word 4) pyramid was built about a thousand years ago in what is now southern Mexico. It stands upon the site of an even older Mayan city known as Chichén Itzá.

7. **hostage**
('häs tij)

(n.) a person held prisoner by another or by an enemy, and used in bargaining for certain demands

The hijacker took one _____hostage_____.

SYNONYMS: a prisoner, pawn

8. **landslide**
('land slīd)

(n.) a fast downhill movement of rocks or soil; any mass that slides down; a lopsided victory in an election

A week of heavy rain caused a _____landslide_____.

SYNONYMS: an avalanche; a rout

9. **rampage**
('ram pāj)

(v.) to rush around wildly or violently

A herd of frightened animals may _____rampage_____.

(n.) violent, reckless, or wild behavior

The news carried a story about looters on a _____rampage_____.

SYNONYMS: to rage; a riot, uproar, turmoil, frenzy

10. **scamper**
('skam pər)

(v.) to run or move quickly or playfully

Children usually _____scamper_____ *around a playground.*

SYNONYMS: to dash, scurry, hurry, scoot, romp
ANTONYMS: to lumber, lag, dawdle, stroll

11. **symptom**
('sim təm)

(n.) a sign of illness or of a physical problem; a sign that something else exists or is happening

Fever is one _____symptom_____ *of the flu.*

SYNONYMS: a signal, clue, indication; evidence

12. **warrant**
('wôr ənt)

(n.) a written order that allows for legal action

The police got a _____warrant_____ *to search the suspect's garage.*

(v.) to declare for certain; to approve or guarantee; to serve as reason for

A deep cut may _____warrant_____ *stitches.*

SYNONYMS: an authorization, guarantee, assurance, permit; to pledge, certify, promise, entitle, authorize, justify

125

For each item below choose the word whose meaning is suggested by the clue given. Then write the word in the space provided.

1. To run happily across a field is to _____scamper_____.
   a. appropriate   b. rampage   c. assemble   d. scamper

2. When you trim a hat with ribbons, you _____adorn_____ it.
   a. appropriate   b. adorn   c. warrant   d. assemble

3. To use something without permission is to _____appropriate_____ it.
   a. rampage   b. warrant   c. appropriate   d. assemble

4. If you have a fever and a rash, you have _____symptoms_____ of measles.
   a. warrants   b. landslides   c. hostages   d. symptoms

5. The date when something begins is its _____effective_____ date.
   a. effective   b. colossal   c. appropriate   d. frail

6. Kidnappers take _____hostages_____ to get money.
   a. warrants   b. hostages   c. landslides   d. symptoms

7. An order that permits the arrest of someone is a _____warrant_____.
   a. warrant   b. rampage   c. landslide   d. symptom

8. The _____colossal_____ skeleton belonged to a gigantic dinosaur.
   a. frail   b. appropriate   c. colossal   d. effective

9. Something that is easily broken is _____frail_____.
   a. effective   b. frail   c. appropriate   d. colossal

10. The reckless actions of a mob may be described as a _____rampage_____.
    a. rampage   b. hostage   c. landslide   d. scamper

11. When you put a model airplane together, you _____assemble_____ it.
    a. warrant   b. appropriate   c. assemble   d. adorn

12. The rocks and mud that block a road are the result of a _____landslide_____.
    a. warrant   b. symptom   c. hostage   d. landslide

Synonyms

For each item below choose the word that is most nearly the **same** in meaning as the word or phrase in **boldface**. Then write your choice on the line provided.

1. **signs** of trouble
   a. warrants   b. hostages   c. landslides   d. symptoms   _____symptoms_____

2. a **pledge** to finish the job
   a. hostage   b. rampage   c. warrant   d. symptom   _____warrant_____

3. communicate with the **prisoner**
   a. rampage   b. landslide   c. symptom   d. hostage   _____hostage_____

4. **rioted** in the streets
   a. rampaged   b. assembled   c. appropriated   d. scampered   _____rampaged_____

5. **ornamented** with jewels
   a. scampered   b. adorned   c. assembled   d. rampaged   _____adorned_____

6. buried by an **avalanche**
   a. hostage   b. landslide   c. symptom   d. warrant   _____landslide_____

Antonyms

For each item below choose the word that is most nearly **opposite** in meaning to the word or phrase in **boldface**. Then write your choice on the line provided.

1. a **robust** person
   a. appropriate   b. frail   c. effective   d. colossal   _____frail_____

2. made a **little** mistake
   a. effective   b. appropriate   c. frail   d. colossal   _____colossal_____

3. **dawdled** on the lawn
   a. scampered   b. warranted   c. adorned   d. assembled   _____scampered_____

4. **unsuitable** clothing for a camping trip
   a. frail   b. effective   c. colossal   d. appropriate   _____appropriate_____

5. a **useless** medicine
   a. frail   b. effective   c. colossal   d. appropriate   _____effective_____

6. where the group will **scatter**
   a. rampage   b. scamper   c. appropriate   d. assemble   _____assemble_____

Completing the Sentence

From the list of words on pages 124–125, choose the one that best completes each item below. Write the word in the space provided. (You may have to change the word's ending.)

A GLORIOUS FOURTH

■ On the Fourth of July, the people who live in our town _____**assemble**_____ peacefully in the park for a picnic and fireworks.

■ Everyone, young and old, comes to the party. Seniors from the high school volunteer to bring people who are too _____**frail**_____ to get to the park on their own.

■ Members of the picnic committee _____**adorn**_____ the trees and the bandstand with red, white, and blue balloons.

■ The band plays patriotic songs and old favorites. People eat and talk, and young children _____**scamper**_____ on the lawns, playing tag and hide-and-seek. Everyone has a wonderful time.

IN HARM'S WAY

■ In wartime invading armies _____**rampage**_____ through cities and towns, destroying everything that lies in their path.

■ The troops _____**appropriate**_____ any food and supplies they want. They may even take over people's homes.

■ A village or an entire region can be held _____**hostage**_____ by the invaders.

■ Such actions _____**warrant**_____ a military response from the defending armies. The victims of the conflict also need aid from international relief agencies.

HOMES AT RISK

■ All along the beautiful coast of California, people build homes on the hills that overlook the ocean. But the _____**colossal**_____ forces of nature can bring danger to those who live on the hillsides.

■ A long period of dry weather is one _____**symptom**_____ that trouble may lie ahead. Dry trees and grasses can easily catch fire. Every year some houses are badly damaged or burn to the ground.

■ When heavy rains come, the homeowners worry about _____**landslides**_____.

■ Even concrete and stone do not always give _____**effective**_____ protection from the power of nature.

Circle the letter next to the word or expression that best completes the sentence or answers the question. Pay special attention to the word in **boldface.**

1. **Effective** exercise helps you
   a. learn to cook
   b. speak Latin
   c. finish your homework
   d. get in shape

2. To **assemble** a jigsaw puzzle, you
   a. lose the pieces
   b. count the pieces
   c. put the pieces back in the box
   d. put the pieces together

3. Which of these is **appropriate** for a dog?
   a. a tennis racket
   b. a library card
   c. a rubber ball
   d. a CD player

4. If we **scamper** in the park, we
   a. drag our feet and moan
   b. skip happily along
   c. ask directions
   d. sit on a bench

5. A **frail** person might
   a. give in to temptation
   b. win a lottery
   c. work for the railroad
   d. stand up for what is right

6. Which is a **symptom** of fear?
   a. giving a brave speech
   b. learning to ride a bike
   c. feeling your heart pound
   d. wearing a scary mask

7. How might a bride **adorn** her wedding gown?
   a. with fabric softener
   b. with pearls and lace
   c. with an apron
   d. with wedding cake

8. It is a **landslide** if you got
   a. 197 votes and I got 5
   b. 150 votes and I got 149
   c. as many votes as I did
   d. elected

9. Most of all, **hostages** want to be
   a. in charge of a party
   b. on vacation
   c. on television
   d. set free

10. If cattle **rampage**, you should
    a. take cover in a safe place
    b. take photographs
    c. sell tickets
    d. blow a whistle

11. A **colossal** tree is likely to be
    a. found in the desert
    b. short and bushy
    c. very tall and thick
    d. home to woodpeckers

12. Carmakers **warrant** that they
    a. always tell the truth
    b. will make repairs as needed
    c. will teach you to drive
    d. can search your car

Selecting Word Meanings

*For each of the following items circle the choice that is most nearly the **same** in meaning as the word in **boldface.***

1. may **warrant** another visit
   a. refuse   (b.) justify   c. request   d. avoid

2. **adopt** a stray kitten
   a. walk   b. abandon   c. brush   (d.) take in

3. the **dominant** idea in the article
   (a.) main   b. silliest   c. only   d. missing

4. expect **courtesy** from the hotel staff
   a. gifts   b. rudeness   (c.) politeness   d. invitations

5. a **drab** scarf
   a. warm   b. long   (c.) dull   d. bright

6. too **frail** to travel
   a. frightened   (b.) sickly   c. busy   d. lazy

7. a **hazardous** mission
   (a.) dangerous   b. secret   c. delicate   d. pointless

8. **noticeable** changes in temperature
   a. uncomfortable   b. sudden   c. slight   (d.) obvious

9. a wild **rampage**
   (a.) frenzy   b. reaction   c. visit   d. dream

10. listened with **genuine** interest
    a. pretended   b. intense   (c.) sincere   d. amused

11. **huddle** by the dim candle
    a. sit   (b.) cluster   c. read   d. gossip

12. **attentive** to details
    a. indifferent   b. drawn   c. faithful   (d.) alert

Spelling

For each item below study the **boldface** word in which there is a blank. If a letter is missing, fill in the blank to make a correctly spelled word. If the word is already spelled correctly, leave the blank empty.

1. a painful **s_y_mptom**

2. an absolute **nec__essity**

3. remarkable **generos_i_ty**

4. a **car_e_free** mood

5. **den_s_e** mist

6. **overth_r_ow** the leaders

7. a sports **ar_e_na**

8. an **a_g_ile** move

9. **analy_z_e** the situation

10. **as_s_emble** the tent

11. a **co__lossal** mess

12. a frightened **hosta_g_e**

Antonyms

For each of the following items circle the choice that is most nearly the **opposite** in meaning to the word in **boldface**.

1. **absolute** knowledge
   a. certain   b. faulty   c. special   (d.) limited

2. a new **ally**
   (a.) opponent   b. partner   c. relative   d. voter

3. **scamper** down the hill
   a. hop   b. roll   (c.) stroll   d. dash

4. **assist** the chef
   a. help   b. blame   c. watch   (d.) hamper

5. **adorn** the stage
   a. decorate   b. build   (c.) damage   d. remove

6. **compliment** her efforts
   (a.) criticize   b. applaud   c. measure   d. reward

7. a **fatal** blow
   (a.) harmless   b. painful   c. deadly   d. shocking

8. **mistrust** my friend
   a. doubt   b. question   c. avoid   (d.) believe

Vocabulary in Context

Words have been left out of the following passage. For each numbered item in the passage, fill in the circle next to the word in the margin that best fills the blank space. Then answer each question below by writing a sentence that contains one of the words you have chosen.

When the new mayor takes office, she will __1__ new people to fill jobs in city government. The mayor is expected to name new deputy mayors and commissioners. She might also choose someone to direct a special community outreach project.

The mayor must conduct a __2__ search for just the right people for the jobs. People who want to work for the mayor must have an interest in the city, strong speaking and writing skills, and a desire to serve the public.

Before offering anyone a job, the mayor and her staff will discuss the __3__ of each candidate. For example, someone who has strong skills but does not get along well with others would be wrong for the job. And a well-liked person with a quick temper could also cause problems.

The mayor will take the time to __4__ her choices carefully. She knows that she must find the best person for each position. And she knows that it is important for the public to respect her judgment. Most of all she needs a team that will serve the city well and make it a better place to live and work.

1. ○ overthrow
   ● appoint
   ○ assist
   ○ offend

2. ● thorough
   ○ peculiar
   ○ carefree
   ○ hazardous

3. ○ symptoms
   ○ courtesies
   ● merits
   ○ allies

4. ○ regain
   ○ adopt
   ○ babble
   ● analyze

5. What will the mayor do before she offers anyone a job?

   The mayor and her staff will discuss the **merits** of each candidate.

6. What must the mayor do to find the right people for the jobs?

   She must conduct a **thorough** search.

7. In what way will the new mayor affect jobs in city goverment?

   She will **appoint** new people to fill available jobs.

8. What will the mayor do to try to make wise choices?

   She will take the time to **analyze** her choices carefully.

**Analogies**
In each of the following circle the letter for the item that best completes the comparison. Then explain the relationship on the lines provided.

1. **captivity** is to **freedom** as
   a. courtesy is to care
   b. fatal is to deadly
   c. noticeable is to obvious
   (d.) abstract is to real

Relationship: *"Captivity" and "freedom"* are antonyms/opposite in meaning; "abstract" and "real" are antonyms/ opposite in meaning.

2. **appropriate** is to **seize** as
   a. overthrow is to support
   b. adopt is to reject
   (c.) scamper is to scurry
   d. merit is to failing

Relationship: *"Appropriate" and "seize"* are synonyms/mean the same; "scamper" and "scurry" are synonyms/mean the same.

3. **peculiar** is to **ordinary** as
   a. rampage is to riot
   (b.) assist is to hinder
   c. regain is to recover
   d. illegal is to criminal

Relationship: *"Peculiar" and "ordinary"* are antonyms/opposite in meaning; "assist" and "hinder" are antonyms/ opposite in meaning.

4. **compliment** is to **good** as
   a. praise is to bad
   b. blame is to good
   (c.) insult is to bad
   d. criticize is to good

Relationship: A compliment makes you feel good; an insult makes you feel bad.

Challenge: Make up your own
Write a comparison using the words in the box below. (Hint: There are three possible analogies.) Then write the relationship on the lines provided.

sand	tiny	enemy	lawn
red	shape	beach	color
colossal	grass	triangle	ally

Analogy: _____ is to _____ as _____ is to _____.

Relationship: See Table of Contents

Word Families

*The words in **boldface** in the sentences below are related to words introduced in Units 13–16. For example, the adjectives ineffective and discourteous in item 1 are related to the adjective effective (Unit 16) and the noun courtesy (Unit 13). Based on your understanding of the unit words that follow, circle the related word in **boldface** that best completes each sentence.*

abstract	effective	captivity	frail	warrant
assist	attentive	agile	compliment	courtesy
deliberate	adorn	fatal	ally	illegal
manufacture	merit	mistrust	offend	analyze

1. This medicine is so old that is it totally (**ineffective**/discourteous).

2. The fiery train crash caused two (**fatalities**/abstractions).

3. The jury's (**deliberations**/illegalities) lasted for five days before a verdict was reached.

4. Regular stretching and exercise can help older people keep some of the (**agility**/frailty) they had when they were young.

5. The Swiss are famous as (assistants/**manufacturers**) of fine watches.

6. The speaker thanked the audience members for their (**attentiveness**/offensiveness).

7. The rooms of the mansion were filled with elegant (warranties/**adornments**).

8. Many family resorts provide (**complimentary**/captive) video games for their guests to enjoy.

9. The United States and Canada have a long-standing (analysis/**alliance**) as trading and defense partners.

10. Three police officers earned medals of honor for (mistrustful/**meritorious**) service to the community.

Word Games

Use the clue and the given letters to complete each word. Write the missing letters of the word in the appropriate boxes. Then use the circled letters and the drawing to answer the CHALLENGE question below.

1. To make a gurgling sound

B (A) B B (L) E

2. Another verb that means "to recover or get back"

R E G A (I) N

3. Thickheaded

(D) E N S E

4. Someone held prisoner

H O (S) T A G (E)

5. Football players do this on the field

H U (D) D (L) E

6. A field of interest, activity, conflict, or debate

A R E (N) A

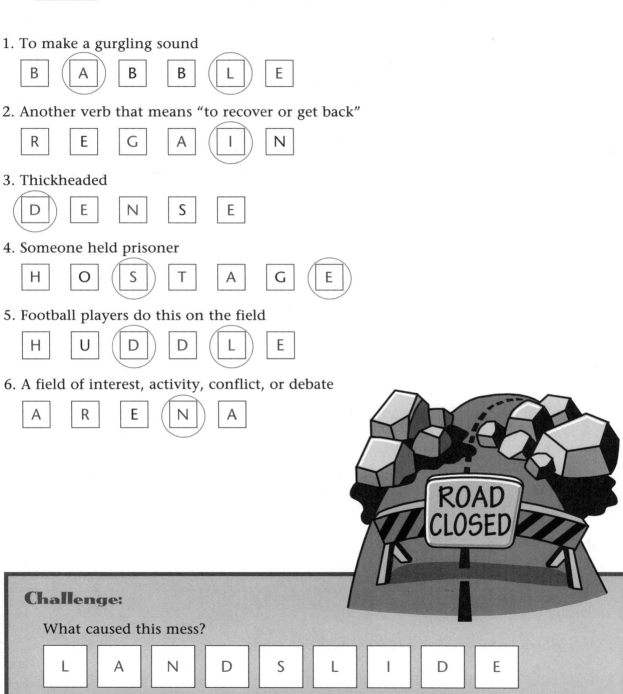

ROAD CLOSED

Challenge:

What caused this mess?

L A N D S L I D E

CUMULATIVE REVIEW II

 **Definitions**

Choose the word from the box that matches each definition. Write the word on the line provided.

adorn	analyze	appoint	colossal	distress
dungeon	focus	generosity	heroic	manufacture
missionary	nourish	offend	peculiar	proceed
provision	quake	regain	toxic	unfit

1. a dark room or cell used as a prison, usually underground   **dungeon**

2. to shake or move back and forth; to tremble   **quake**

3. the quality of being charitable to others   **generosity**

4. to make something, especially using machinery   **manufacture**

5. not physically or mentally healthy   **unfit**

6. to feed or help grow and develop; to support   **nourish**

7. to cause hurt feelings, anger, or injury   **offend**

8. brave, noble, or larger than life   **heroic**

9. to go on or continue; to start again after a pause   **proceed**

10. to study carefully or in detail   **analyze**

11. a step taken ahead of time; a condition, as in a contract   **provision**

12. odd or curious; not like the normal or usual   **peculiar**

13. poisonous or deadly   **toxic**

14. deep worry or suffering; being in danger or trouble   **distress**

15. amazingly large, great, or powerful   **colossal**

 **Antonyms** *Choose the word from the box that is most nearly* **opposite** *in meaning to each group of words. Write the word on the line provided.*

1. ordinary, regular, usual, average   outstanding

2. to criticize, insult, denounce   compliment

3. gentle, refined, polite   coarse

4. freshwater, land   marine

5. smooth, even, regular   jagged

6. to reject, disown, abandon   adopt

7. a penalty, deduction, fine   bonus

8. to scatter, break up, disperse   assemble

9. faith, hope, trust, confidence   despair

10. actual, real, physical, concrete   abstract

11. to acquit, free, release   convict

12. alert, clever, smart   dense

13. overlooked, hidden, obscure   noticeable

14. insincere, trivial, frivolous, foolish   earnest

15. to disgrace, demote, lower   elevate

16. an option, extra, luxury   necessity

17. freedom, independence, liberty   captivity

18. to lumber, lag, dawdle, stroll   scamper

19. early, prompt, on time   tardy

20. to parch, dry   drench

abstract
adopt
assemble
bonus
captivity
coarse
compliment
convict
dense
despair
drench
earnest
elevate
fatal
jagged
marine
necessity
noticeable
outstanding
register
scamper
site
tardy
variety
warrant

Completing the Sentence

Choose the word from the box that best completes each sentence below. Write the word in the space provided.

Group A

discard	extraordinary	grumble	inspire
pointless	sift	spree	uneasy

1. My dad may _____**grumble**_____ about it, but he always walks our dog at night.

2. Many people feel _____**uneasy**_____ about traveling in stormy weather.

3. It took hours for my mom to _____**sift**_____ through that big pile of old magazines, but she enjoyed the task.

4. She found a(n) _____**extraordinary**_____ number of magazines with stories about the rich and the famous.

5. By the end of the afternoon, Mom decided to _____**discard**_____ all but two of the magazines.

Group B

absolute	ally	genuine	huddle
illegal	landslides	overthrow	symptom

1. Public protests have led to the _____**overthrow**_____ of cruel and corrupt rulers throughout history.

2. In many cases people were outraged that their rulers made _____**illegal**_____ use of tax money to buy luxuries while many citizens lived in poverty.

3. Rebels have refused to allow such rulers to continue to have _____**absolute**_____ control over all areas of people's lives.

4. When free elections have been held, representatives of the people have won by overwhelming _____**landslides**_____.

5. Such democratic victories have given people _____**genuine**_____ opportunities to lead better lives.

Classifying *Choose the word from the box that goes best with each group of words. Write the word in the space provided. Then explain what the words have in common.*

arena	bristle	chant	circular	drab
juvenile	mistrust	reflect	site	treaty

1. beige, tan, gray, _____ drab _____

   The words name dull colors.

2. whisker, spine, quill, _____ bristle _____

   The words name things that are short and stiff.

3. carol, hymn, _____ chant _____

   The words describe kinds of song.

4. infant, _____ juvenile _____, adult

   The words name different stages of growth.

5. _____ reflect _____, reflection, reflective, reflector

   The words belong to the same family.

6. leaflet, pamphlet, flyer, advertisement, _____ circular _____

   The words name kinds of printed material.

7. stadium, auditorium, _____ arena _____, theater

   The words name an enclosed space for sports or shows.

8. sight, _____ site _____, cite

   The words are spelled differently but sound the same.

9. pact, accord, _____ treaty _____

   The words are synonyms.

10. misfit, misprint, mislead, _____ mistrust _____

    The words begin with the same prefix.

FINAL MASTERY TEST

Definitions *For each item choose the word that matches the definition. Then write the word on the line provided.*

1. to close off or keep people or supplies from going in or out
   a. dungeon   b. enclose   c. grasp   (d.) blockade   <u>blockade</u>

2. changing little by little
   (a.) gradual   b. jagged   c. unfit   d. agile   <u>gradual</u>

3. lack of sameness; a category of plants or animals
   a. spree   (b.) variety   c. mission   d. extreme   <u>variety</u>

4. to unite or join for a special purpose
   a. adorn   b. adopt   (c.) ally   d. assist   <u>ally</u>

5. to guide, excite, uplift, or encourage
   (a.) inspire   b. focus   c. magnify   d. reflect   <u>inspire</u>

6. done or said on purpose; at a slow or steady pace
   a. thorough   b. hazardous   c. dense   (d.) deliberate   <u>deliberate</u>

7. a quality that deserves reward or praise
   a. mistrust   (b.) merit   c. symptom   d. haste   <u>merit</u>

8. to take over or use as one's own, often without permission
   a. compliment   b. warrant   (c.) appropriate   d. sift   <u>appropriate</u>

9. in great supply, easily available; more than enough
   a. alert   b. awkward   (c.) plentiful   d. tidy   <u>plentiful</u>

10. a widespread outbreak of disease; sudden rapid growth
    (a.) epidemic   b. ancestor   c. noble   d. policy   <u>epidemic</u>

11. to draw attention to something else; to confuse or disturb
    a. blossom   (b.) distract   c. dismiss   d. survive   <u>distract</u>

12. to set up, start, organize, or bring about; to prove beyond doubt
    a. appoint   b. assemble   c. rampage   (d.) establish   <u>establish</u>

13. beginning or first

    a. annual   b. sturdy   c. urgent   (d.) initial   _____ initial _____

14. a load; something that is very hard to bear

    a. pledge   b. sponsor   (c.) burden   d. stampede   _____ burden _____

15. not used, filled, or lived in; without thought or expression

    (a.) vacant   b. suitable   c. content   d. foul   _____ vacant _____

16. honest and truthful

    a. gallant   (b.) sincere   c. weary   d. abstract   _____ sincere _____

17. having no meaning or effect

    a. tardy   (b.) pointless   c. uneasy   d. dominant   _____ pointless _____

18. to get back; to reach again

    a. overthrow   b. nourish   c. provision   (d.) regain   _____ regain _____

19. a lively or wild outburst of activity

    (a.) spree   b. chant   c. juvenile   d. treaty   _____ spree _____

20. a major product, material, part, or item regularly used

    a. ration   b. drought   (c.) staple   d. routine   _____ staple _____

Part of Speech

*For each item below indicate the part of speech of the word in **boldface**. In the space provided write N for noun, V for verb, or A for adjective.*

21. _V_ **discipline** the puppy   26. _N_ join the **huddle**

22. _N_ the election **register**   27. _V_ **babble** on for hours

23. _V_ **lance** the infection   28. _A_ **effective** on insect bites

24. _A_ **troublesome** tasks   29. _N_ a generous **portion**

25. _A_ **attentive** to my wishes   30. _V_ **trudge** home from work

Completing the Sentence

Choose the word from the box that best completes each sentence. Write the word in the space provided. (You may have to change the word's ending.)

Group A

appoint	carefree	collide	enclose
extend	feeble	magnify	response

31. My aunt wears special glasses that can _____ **magnify** _____ small print.

32. Don't forget to _____ **enclose** _____ a gift card inside the box so that the bride will know who sent her the present.

33. The President will _____ **appoint** _____ ambassadors and members of the cabinet.

34. It is always a treat to find that you have a _____ **carefree** _____ afternoon ahead of you with no chores or homework to do.

Group B

adorn	clatter	demonstrate	dominant
employ	toxic	sensible	sponsor

35. Blue, green, and purple are the _____ **dominant** _____ colors in my wardrobe.

36. Even a small amount of shellfish can be _____ **toxic** _____ to someone who is very allergic to it.

37. For our Fourth of July picnic, we will _____ **adorn** _____ the tables and the yard with flags and red, white, and blue flowers.

38. The _____ **sponsor** _____ of our soccer team donated money for uniforms, equipment, and trophies.

*Circle the letter next to the word or expression that best completes the sentence or answers the question. Pay special attention to the word in **boldface**.*

39. A family might **dwell** in
    a. an apartment
    b. a teakettle
    c. a magazine
    d. a videotape

40. It is a **courtesy** to
    a. make fun of me
    b. finish my dessert
    c. climb my ladder
    d. open a door for me

41. A **frail** person is
    a. strong
    b. weak
    c. wise
    d. jumpy

42. In **extreme** heat, I might
    a. turn on the furnace
    b. eat a heavy meal
    c. wear light clothing
    d. clean out the attic

43. Which is a **disaster**?
    a. the hiccups
    b. an earthquake
    c. a rainbow
    d. a book report

44. To **lash** signs to a fence,
    a. use rope
    b. use glue
    c. use water
    d. use paint

45. A **scholar** does a lot of
    a. singing
    b. skating
    c. studying
    d. spying

46. To plan an **ambush**, find a
    a. good book
    b. flowerpot
    c. tall chair
    d. hiding spot

47. A sore toe might **indicate**
    a. an infection
    b. nail polish
    c. comfortable shoes
    d. new socks

48. Many **hazardous** tools are
    a. flat
    b. new
    c. sharp
    d. squishy

49. Most people **recall**
    a. a recipe for pumpkin pie
    b. their own birthday
    c. all the state capitals
    d. how to play polo

50. To do a **thorough** cleaning,
    a. be sure to wash the dishes
    b. be sure to paint the doors
    c. be sure to sweep the halls
    d. be sure to scrub everything

INDEX

The following is a list of all the words taught in the units of this book. The number after each entry indicates the page on which the word is first introduced, but the word also appears in exercises on later pages.

absolute, 112
abstract, 106
accurate, 54
adopt, 118
adorn, 124
agile, 118
alert, 54
ally, 106
ambush, 30
analyze, 118
ancestor, 54
annual, 18
antique, 42
appoint, 106
appropriate, 124
arena, 112
assemble, 124
assist, 118
attentive, 106
attractive, 24
awkward, 60

babble, 118
baggage, 42
basic, 18
blockade, 88
blossom, 48
bonus, 106
bristle, 94
burden, 24

calculate, 30
captivity, 118
carefree, 107
celebrity, 12
chant, 88
circular, 94
clatter, 60
coarse, 94
collide, 48
colossal, 124
competition, 18
compliment, 112

consent, 24
constant, 48
content, 48
contract, 18
contribute, 25
convict, 76
counsel, 12
courtesy, 106

deliberate, 112
demonstrate, 12
dense, 112
dependable, 24
despair, 88
digest, 42
disaster, 54
discard, 94
discipline, 76
dismiss, 18
distract, 48
distress, 82
dominant, 112
drab, 119
dread, 30
drench, 82
drought, 48
drowsy, 12
dungeon, 76
dwell, 82

earnest, 76
effective, 124
elementary, 54
elevate, 88
employ, 30
enclose, 76
envy, 54
epidemic, 55
essential, 12
establish, 42
eternal, 42
extend, 30
extraordinary, 88
extreme, 94

fatal, 119
feeble, 55
focus, 94
foul, 49
frail, 124
frantic, 31

gallant, 60
generosity, 119
genuine, 119
gradual, 76
grasp, 95
grumble, 77

hardship, 12
haste, 42
haul, 13
hazardous, 113
heroic, 88
hostage, 125
huddle, 113
humble, 13
humid, 43

illegal, 119
indicate, 24
initial, 31
inspire, 95

jagged, 77
juvenile, 82

lance, 89
landslide, 125
lash, 43
lukewarm, 60

magnify, 95
manufacture, 107
marine, 95
merit, 119
missionary, 89
mistrust, 107

necessity, 113
neglect, 18
noble, 49
noticeable, 107
nourish, 77

obtain, 19
offend, 113
oppose, 43
outstanding, 82
overthrow, 107

peculiar, 107
penetrate, 55
pioneer, 43
pledge, 13
plentiful, 60
pointless, 89
policy, 49
portion, 19
previous, 24
proceed, 82
provision, 77

quake, 95
qualify, 25
quiver, 49

rampage, 125
ration, 60
recall, 19
reflect, 89
regain, 113
register, 83
reserve, 61
response, 25
romp, 55
routine, 31

scamper, 125
scholar, 61
sensible, 43
shabby, 25

sift, 83
sincere, 13
site, 89
slight, 49
smolder, 61
sponsor, 19
spree, 83
stampede, 13
staple, 55
stern, 19
stun, 31
sturdy, 31
suitable, 13
survive, 55
symptom, 125

tardy, 83
thaw, 25
thorough, 113
tidy, 49
toxic, 89
treaty, 77
troublesome, 95
trudge, 61

uneasy, 77
unfit, 83
urgent, 25

vacant, 19
vanity, 25
variety, 83
volunteer, 61

warrant, 125
weary, 61
worthy, 43

yield, 31